WORK *Welfare* the *& Price of* FISH

Life in Aberdeen
1925-1955

Project Leader: **David Atherton.**
Researcher: **Trevor Davies.**

Introduction

This book was initiated partly by Councillor David Clyne's suggestion "That the Council mark the 50th anniversary of the end of the Second World War", and partly to commemorate the 125th anniversary of the Trades Council. Through these reminiscences, Aberdeen folk graphically portray not only their working experiences but also personal feelings with regard to their lives' political or otherwise.

Against the grim background of pawnshops, soupkitchens and particularly the 'Means Test', many folk struggled with resilience on meagre wages and 'buroo' (bureau) to survive a period that saw both depression and war; where the commonplace was poverty and unemployment. These reminiscences not only characterise this stoicism but also reflect the political idealism that emerged as a response to what people saw as an unfair system. This militancy against injustice was international and resulted in such phenomena as the Aberdeen Hunger March at home, and the fight against Fascism, firstly with the Spanish Civil War and later with the Second World War in the world at large.

With the ending of the Second World War there was an optimism leading to a feeling that ordinary people could effect change and it was with this notion that many voted Labour in 1945. The ensuing landslide victory made real some of their hopes and aspirations many of which were embodied in the creation of the Welfare State.

Old dwellings at 16 Shiprow 1920s

Part one

Aberdeen during the Slump

John Londragan: Aberdeen during the 1930's was best remembered for its industrial scene, all the people who were involved lived cheek by jowl with industry and when they met in the pubs all they talked about was their industry an' all that and how things were an' that. That's the kind of conversation.

There were the old pubs with the rail and sawdust on the floor. There were nae seats, they were nae needin' tae sit, they'd come in tae drink!

At that time most o' the industries finished at half past five to six o'clock, particularly the fishin' industry where the girls working in the arches and Torry and so forth, - they finished their work. And all the streets were cobbled, there were no such things as tar Macadam then, and when they finished their work, comin' home all the larries which carried the fish through the day through the fish houses and back from the harbour up to the fish houses an' so forth, - workin' all day back an' forth. They finished at half-past five and the girls all piled on to the larries, - and you'd hear the sound away reachin, - you'd stand in the Castlegate, stand in the Gallowgate and you'd hear the sound startin' and they'd say that's the girls comin' home and this was the larries with the iron tyres an' that thumpin' on the cassies and the horses come up Market Street and turnin' 'em up towards the Castlegate and down King Street an' distribute to different areas where they dropped their load, a' the girls an' so forth an' dockers an' what not, - to the different areas where they stayed because they'd no transport, - well transport was too dear for them even at a penny a time, and they used to come like that. And hundreds o' lorries used to come up Market street and along Union street and down King Street and so forth. The noise built up, they were racin' for home nae walkin', they used to race for home because the driver wanted to get finished also. There'd be accidents there also, many a lamp post was knocked over with the lorries an' that ...

With this noise element from the trains an' everything the whole thing just piled up and people would find it incredulous to think in terms o' the noise that was involved, and yet, you didn't hear it. Because it was a cloud o' noise, it was always there and when you came out in the evenings when work was all finished an' that, it was a totally different Aberdeen after the workin' day and 'rush-hour'. Everything was quiet, very few firms were workin' late at night an' that there. It would give you a chance to hear the speakers in the Castlegate!

Albion Street from Park Street

Albion Street looking West from Hanover Lane

John L: My father and his two brothers were in the Navy in the First World War. When they came back he worked in the docks with the Aberdeen Coal Company later on, but he was three years idle to begin with. He got a job back in the docks again because the people workin' in the docks already carried on workin' there. There was no protection for jobs then and this happened in hundreds o' cases. I have the visual pictures of the men and the desolation on their faces and everything y'know. Standin' on street corners and that there. Not knowin' what to do they had nowhere to express themselves for that. That came later on with the General Strike. The General Strike was the start o' the opposition an' fightin' back but up until that time they felt that there was nothing they could do. There were demonstrations led by the Trades Council and by the different unions and that up and down the street. I remember the class o' policemen we had at that time. In these days they took the biggest, the ugliest, and the heaviest built country men they could find. They recruited at Skene, Oldmeldrum and Elgin and they took them doon here and honestly, I don't mean to describe them as actually dumb altogether but that's the impression y'got. There was nothing in between here (indicating his head) absolutely nothing at all (laughter) and they jist stood at the corner there with their batons, all with their batons in their hands and so forth this was the warnin' an' they went about in pairs an' that.

Alex Collie: It's strange how you remember some things and not others but I thought this was so funny, I'll never forget it. Well in those days, horses were worked until they dropped. Well, one day I wis walkin' along Constitution Street and this poor horse had collapsed. There wis nae protection league in those days, well not that I wis aware of. Well, a bobby comes along and at 'at time they were powerful big brozey men and not so literate as they might be. He wis taken doon the particulars of this incident asking the relevant questions like "Where were you going with the horse, what were y' doin'?" an' things like that. An' then he sez, "Fit street's es?" "Oh, it's Constitution Street." sez the other. Well, the bobby mused till himself for a few seconds knowing that he couldna' spell Constitution, then he said, "Could y' jist pull the horse roond the corner here t' Park Street!

John Londragan: I remember, as a young lad, living in West North Street and at the far end o' West North Street near King Street there was where the 'hawkers' lived. The hawkers were the buran (sic) gypsies, we called them 'hackers' they were travellin' people. That was 6 West North Street next to the 'Hairy Bar', they lived there one room at the weekend, they would all come together at the weekend and there would a' been sixteen or seventeen livin' in one room all at the weekend before they dispersed on the Monday. And the red wine was on the go, the red wine was the thing at that time with the drinkers. All the kids would come down even the women and that they would all come down at the bottom o' Little John Street, they would all stand there, they knew what was going to happen. At about half past eight before the pubs closed and so forth the doors of this house would open up an' all the men would come oot, the drunks, they'd all come oot. They all walked in tackety boots, nobody wore anything else but tackety boots in those days. Heavy boots wi' steel studs in em and they'd walk up the road an' there was six policemen stan'in' across the top o' West North Street their batons in their hand and the two 'Black Marias' roond the corner in Queen Street. And this was a Saturday night event,

Longacre looking towards West North Street - 1924

like goin' t' the pictures and these lads would come oot and they'd look up and see them and they'd start cat callin' names and to show them how strong they were they'd walk up to the granite dyke o' the Marischal College and they'd run their feet along the wall and you'd a seen the sparks flyin' along the granite afore they challenged the bobbies then they'd march up the road towards the bobbies, fourteen or fifteen o' them then the doors o' the vans, the 'Black Marias' would open up an' the police would pour oot and the whole lot o them would come oot. Then there was a melee for aboot half an hoor or so and they would spend the rest o' the weekend in gaol and they were released on the Monday and that happened every weekend an' this sort o' pantomime went on all the time y' know along wi' the different characters in the toon at that time.

Housing conditions for working class folk in Aberdeen

John Londragan: If ye were to stick a pin in a map, and draw a circle half-a-mile from the centre that was Aberdeen in the 1920's and '30's. There was nothing beyond that except farmland.

The exodus of the people started after the Second World War and the factories took over the centre of the town and the people were moved to the outskirts.

Mat Davidson: There was a street in Aberdeen name o' Wales Street, which is the Boulevard now. They reckoned that when Wales Street emptied it took two housing schemes to accommodate all the people. The average family was about six people. If ye think, there was maybe eight people banged up in two rooms, they might get a four or five room hoose.

John L: There was seven tenants in oor hoose and that was 84 people! There was two toilets, both outside.

Mat: There was a story, I reckon it was true, that Rennie the butcher in East North Street, there was a tenement next door, there were no tenants on the ground-floor because of the butcher's and the hairdresser's, and there was 59 people in the upstairs with one toilet. And that wasn't unusual.

When we lived in Frederick Street, there was Clark's up the stair, the fireman lived up the stair, there was the grandmother and others. There was only one toilet in that hoose, and every

Top: Wales Street from Park Street
Centre: Shuttle Lane from Shuttle Court - 1927
Bottom: East North Street - 1915

day without fail, yer mither would make two, three journeys up and down stairs with the pail. It was a way of life and ye niver thocht onything o' it. If Her Majesty had come into the house, yer mither would have gone on with the pail, it was just part of her duties.

Wm. Simpson: Look here, you'd come into the house, and there'd be the sink, there'd be nae cooker, the fire would be here, it might be a range, but we just had a fire. That would be yer livin'-room, and then you'd have yer best room, and also the kid's bedroom. The three of us, George and I and my sister all slept in the same bedroom, when we got older, my mother discovered she had a cousin who stayed near by, and she got us this flat which had two bedrooms. George and I slept in the small bedroom, and the sister slept in that other bedroom cum best room. The other room was just the same as in the other tenement.

John Lennox: The Street where I grew up in Aberdeen, down near the shipyards, was only a short street. There were seven blocks of tenements, six houses - room and kitchen - to each block. The families were a' big in those days. We had six in our family and faither and mother was eight. The Pratt's was fourteen o' a family - seven of that men. So there was a lot o' men folk in our street but oot of all the menfolk there was only three that was working; Pratt and McCallum worked in the docks, and my father was a butcher.

John Londragan: The housin' situation was the worst one o' the whole lot. The city manager at that time, he was a hell o' a nice lad, Dawson, Mr. Dawson, he was too good for the job, he was willin' to listen to everybody and that was his bloody downfall. In that sort o' job you can't do it you have to play by the rule and not get emotionally involved. He had two clerks in the front office, the people were lined up the stairs an' so forth about houses, gettin' houses, gettin' this repaired and all the rest o' it and the clerks would just throw up their bloody hands you know, they got that fed up wi' it and if somebody managed to get past the clerks and get an interview with Dawson, which was a great thing if you got an interview with Dawson because that was the top of the ladder you could get nae further the King was the next one up frae that! And you would go in there, Dawson, give him his due he would listen to everybody, but it was a hell of a job for him.

Things got so bad in the '30's particularly after the depression people didn't have money even for a *controlled rent because the men were out of work, the depression was that bad and most o' the houses in Aberdeen were private property. The result was that the landlords were going to turf them out, they'd nowhere to go, so the complaints were coming in so fast that I,

Top: Shepherd's Court, 21 Guestrow
Bottom: Top of the Gallowgate

4

along with a lot o' young lads saw what was happenin' and said we'll have to see if we can do something to help the people an' that so we would go along to the people and see who's affected. They'd say we've been given our notice from the landlord we've got to be out next week an' that and so forth. We'd say 'ok' then and we'd lay out certain dates for them to be comin' out. In the meantime we'd go round the empty private properties lying about Aberdeen here, and there was a lot at that particular time. Some of them were in a poor condition I'd agree never the less they were houses and we would go along there - they were chained up and locked an' all the rest o'it so we'd unlock 'em and bust the chains an' that and go inside to see if they were fit for human habitation - you wouldn't keep dogs in 'em when you look back on it! But at that particular time a house was a bloody house, so we examined 'em an' all that and found they were all recht then we'd count how many families we could get in may be six or seven families, it depends on the size o' the house in fact one o' the buildin's the very top o' Young Street we got fifteen families in I remember that. Fifteen families is an average of just over a hundred people.

The controlled rent was a means by which the council regulated the rents of tenants who were on low incomes. The scheme of rebates were proposed in 1937. Generally speaking, the sum equal to one sixth of the average weekly income of the household would be regarded as the basis of the amount to be charged by way of rent.

We'd down to Cocky Hunter's, then, - before we did that we'd go back and tell the families what we're goin' to do, and to get all the furniture ready and we'd move it, and then we'd go down to Cocky Hunter's and it would cost us sixpence a time fa' Cocky Hunter t' get a barra - a small handcart y'know. We'd get half a dozen o'them dependin' on how many people were movin' at a time, it cost us sixpence for the use of the barra for a forenoon or an afternoon. We'd g' doon with the barras pile a' the furniture on till it, whip em along to East North Street and along West North Street or roond the corner t' the Gallowgate on t' the top there.

The boys 'ud be there with the doors already open there, nobody knew anything about it, it was kept very quiet and under cover an' that - the Intelligence on the go! We'd empty a' the barras, take the families in an' show 'em the rooms, tek up the furniture an' everything an' put it all in. Sometimes they didn't have water or anything like that. It was all turned off because they were derelict buildings, y'see they'd turn off the water and the gas, there was no electricity. Never the less we put the people in, after we put them in the spare boys goin' aboot tekin' the barras away out o' the road an' a' that there, we'd stick a table oot side, by this time it would be gettin' towards evening, the men and the women had their suppers an' that there. After they had their meals we'd get the table oot stand upon the table, with megaphones we'd tell all

Top: Press criticism of Council Housing Policies - 1935
Centre: Shoe Lane looking from West North Street
Bottom: Adverts for 'Cocky' Hunter - 1932

the people and they'd come doon t' see what all the trouble was an' that, and we'd explain what had happened to them, these people were homeless, and had been thrown out of their homes and the men canna get work.

Then we'd go down town, we'd already phoned Mr. Dawson beforehand and told him we'd be there to meet him at about half past eight in the evening. And sure enough, he'd be there, and we'd ask him to protect the people who was in, because sometimes the council, got very irritated and would send the police up and try and cause evictions y' know and the only people who could defy the police was the people themselves with the help of the people about them. We left, and the people about them took over. They gathered at the buildin' and went in and gave them water 'cause there was no water. They gave them heatin', paraffin lamps and all the rest o' it, and even food an' so forth.

We goes doon tae see Dawson and I tells him what we've done an' that. "Now it's your problem, it's your property," and I says, "These people are living there and if you are going to evict them you are going to have trouble on your hands, I'm tellin' you." And he took it to heart, he knew bloody well there'd be trouble because the last thing the council wanted at that particular time was to cause more trouble. With the depression at its height y'know, there were so many things boilin' over the top and at the same time the political impetus and the fact that there were only about four Labour seats in the whole of the town council and this was a threat if they didn't give satisfaction to people as regards a house and so forth, would lead to the Tory councillors losing their seats as they actually did at the end of 1938 and 1939 most of the Tory councils were out. But any how, we put it to Dawson, an' he said, "ok", so it was only a couple o' days after when the workmen come up and sorted the roof, put in water put on the gas and a' the rest o' it.

At the same time we collected the rent. We collected the rent from the people. And sometimes they didn't have money but nevertheless we chipped in an' a' the rest o' it, we got the money for them, an' after the first fortnight they were in then we went down to the council and paid the rent for 'em. They were adopted as council tenants. This is the sort o' thing the poor helpin' the poor, there was nobody else to help 'em.

Justice Lane

Even on the basis o' enjoyin' themselves they only had two places in Aberdeen where they could enjoy themselves one was the Gallowgate, the pitches, and it was here that the young kids, that is to say from the early school age right up until about fourteen year old, would come to the pitches there and form themselves into football teams and so forth and this kept them occupied in the evenin' there was no question o' goin' to cafés an' things like that, we didn't have cafés, we didn't have money in the first place. So the kids kept themselves occupied with the sort o' physical activity an' that there. The other young people, say from about sixteen, fourteen, fifteen, sixteen up until the middle age for that matter they used to do the same thing but they used to go to the Aulton links that's where the juvenile football was played an' that and the young men who would have been the radical element at that particular time, they would be involved in the football and so forth there.

Alex Collie: We hid a team down there, the bakery workers, the Wednesday league, and the Wednesday league wis a the shop assistants who hid the half days - people wid be off at that time - it was a Wednesday league. Now there wis a lot of people, has-beens' and so on like this.... what tickled me about them was being so small against the cumbersome, heavy boys, whose legs - well I know what it is now, they hardly move - bit when you're rinning aboot, they liked entertainment, you know, virtually making a fool - football wise of course - with the players from the different teams. Generally people enjoyed their football. Of course it wis ashes (The playing area) and so on doon there.

Later on there wis an opportunity there, there wis a difficulty aboot getting a ball,

Top: Woman using outdoor tap
Bottom: Wales Street from Hanover Street

and eh, what they did was they took up a collection, if you paid into the collection you got a game. So I was paid into the collection. Now, listen to this, they hired a ball from Cockey Hunters for a shilling. So I stood a good chance of getting a game wi my penny! That's a fact!

Noo, that ball was aboot that thick (Gestures it at approx $\frac{1}{2}$ an inch) in patches, it wis that! Kicking it wis like hitting a steel ball.

Ted Munro: You couldna heed it, you took concussion!

John Londragan: Even with all that activities goin' on y' still had hundreds of people comin' round the Castlegate there listenin' to the speakers an' that an' at two, three o'clock in the mornin' the bobbies would come along, country bobbies they were, at that time, - you were engaged as a policeman for your height, for your build and for the fact that you come from the country, so you know nothin' about the town, there was no emotional connection with the town at all. The result was that the bobbies would come on the scene and stand by there, and about three o'clock in the mornin' they'd start sayin' to people "It's about time you were goin home" an that. There were still crowds o' people at three o'clock in the mornin' in groups there, discussin' things an' that - a militancy existed in the people that we cannot conceive now at the present time.

David: What attracted you to the Independent Labour Party? (The I.L.P.)

Bill Morrice: At that time y'know, I mean, oor mothers were mainly slaves a' their lives, y'know. The conditions they lived under, the whole set up, the I.L.P. was the left wing o' the Labour Party - they were propoundin' socialism, an' fight for better rights, better housin' an' onything like 'at because at that time housin' was terrible an' they were the ones that spear heeded this struggle.

Jimmy Reid: Well I was brought up in Wales Street actually, St. Clement's ward. That was a Communist area. As I say, I was lucky, ma father had a good job an' we rented the house at the bottom o' Wales Street which was a reasonably good house - we had water in the house, well, we'd a sink! Most o' the houses at the bottom o' Wales Street there, had either the sinks in the landin' or you had your tap outside.

Alex Collie: Conditions an that, that the people doon there in Fittie lived. I hid an application in (for re-housing) which I never pursued when I saw fit happened doon there. I wis lucky, I wis living at Mansefield Road.

Another time we went down t' look at this house in Virginia Street. Good God I never realised that it could be so bad it was a little wee place wi hardly any light reachin' it, so little that it wis pitch dark in there wi the sun shining bright outside! I came across the family sittin' in the door. Workin' class people often sat at the door to hae a news but wi these folk it was more for the lack o' light! When I saw this I decided I should get them oota there as quick as possible. One thing that struck me forcibly was as soon as you re-housed someone you created a dissatisfied person because nearly all folk wanted out of poor housing so the people that were left behind were still living in bad conditions and I always regretted that it was not possible to re-house them all. However, some of the accommodation we then built was also later to be seen as unsuitable. What we did, sadly, was to help kill the community but it's difficult to see ahead.

UNEMPLOYMENT AND THE POOR

"There'd be queues of men at the Labour Exchange fighting to get a shovel to clear the snow."

John Londragan: Everybody was involved in the slump, the effects were horrendous in this country. As far as we were concerned, political anger was being demonstrated not just against the fact that they had been sacked but the reasons why you had been sacked an' that. The political intelligence of the people now began to increase they began to see that there was something they could do about it.

Mrs Nicol: I must have been about ten before I would take notice, (of education) but the unemployment was terrible. There was no work for the men and this affected everybody. There was no money and the poverty was terrible. They would try to get work doin' odd jobs but there was nothin'. Even educated people were unemployed, there was just no work for them. When I look back on the struggle for existence, I have to admire the parents. Some of my chums, girls of 13 and 14, their parents would have to go to the Public Assistance and they got very little help.

Demands for Increased Relief
Council Hears N.U.W.M. Deputation

DEMANDS for increased relief for the unemployed and the inauguration of work schemes at trade union rates and conditions were made of Aberdeen Town Council on Monday by a deputation of the local branch of the National Unemployed Workers' Movement.

The demands, which were supported by a number of trade unions and the Trades and Labour Council, were:—Increased relief of 3s for each dependent child; the restoration of cuts in public assistance and transitional benefits; 25 per cent. reduction in rents of municipal houses; extra winter relief in the form of boots, coal, clothing, etc.; and the closing of working class streets to traffic.

The deputation stated that, in view of centralisation of industry, Aberdeen would be left in the backwater. The only hope for the future was to develop the city as a health resort, and that did not simply mean an improvement of the beach, but re-conditioning the streets. If all the work schemes mooted by the Council were adopted, there would be a shortage of workers instead of a surplus.

It was also pointed out that the Medical Officer of Health had revealed that a considerable proportion of school children were suffering from malnutrition and were badly clothed. The reason was that their parents were not receiving adequate relief. This was considered to be a disgrace.

MORE RELIEF FOR CHILDREN.

A woman member of the deputation said that an extra allowance for the children was necessary, particularly in the winter. She pointed out that children required medicine, and in her view every child should have a pint of milk a day. This ran away with 1s 9d of the 2s relief. Parents were left with 3d to provide all the other necessaries.

Another woman complained that two feeding centres were not sufficient. When the deputation had withdrawn, several members of the Council asked for prompt consideration of the demands. Re

An allegation that the Joiners and Carpenters' Association was trying to force the hand of the Council was made by Councillor Morrison, convener of the Housing Committee, when he recommended that the Council should not consider the carpenters' tenders for new houses, and that they should invite fresh tenders, if necessary, outside the city.

In the minutes of the Housing Committee it was reported that when tenders were originally invited, the condition was laid down that they should be on a firm

Lily Morris, the great music hall favourite, appears at the Tivoli next week.

Newspaper cutting highlighting fears for the unemployed

John Lennox: The National Unemployment Workers Movement was quite strong in Aberdeen. They had an old church hall. The N.U.W.M. got the rent fairly cheap. It was quite a good place but it was a bit dilapidated. After all, life was a bit dilapidated in these days. People wernae used to the plushy lights and the standards nowadays. But the N.U.W.M. hall was a focus, people were attracted there. Anybody who had a claim or was in trouble they come to the N.U.W.M. wi' their cases. Johny Mackie took up the cases for the unemployed.

Johnny was ages wi' me, I suppose. He was a tubby sort o' man and he was flat footed so Johnny could never have gone on the Hunger March: he had enough to do to cross the road as far as walking was concerned. But he had a fatherly kind of appearance. He had left the school at fourteen same as me so he didnae hae the advantage o' a higher education or anything like that. But he took up the cases of the unemployed and acted as a councillor for the workers. And by gosh he got results. It was petty, the sums involved, but it meant an awfa lot to the people involved. Johnny wasnae an N.U.W.M. organiser and couldna have gone on a platform. He jist was a worker and he jist had the knack of being able to present people's cases and get an understanding about the whole thing.

On social occasions at the N.U.W.M. hall it was really remarkable. The jiggin', the dancin', was right popular - many of the best dancers in town went! Well, ye could say the unemployed got plenty o' time to practice! They got quite a good band together. So these unemployed fellows learned to dance and they could go up the town and at the Palais de Danse they could have held their own wi' the best o' them.

I forget exactly but it was only fourpence (1.5p) or something like that to get into the N.U.W.M. jiggin'. So it didnae kill anybody if they wanted to dance. As a result we had a lot o' activities and this funded the other activities of the N.U.W.M. Now, there was nobody made a fortune, it was jist a mountain o' pennies really, ye were dealin' in coppers. In a lot o' ways, while it was hard to come by money you could live on the cheap. Across the road from the hall was a chipper and you could get a chip supper for four old pence - about 1.5 new pence. But that was the foundation o' the N.U.W.M. That was why it was so successful in Aberdeen. Now that's where the 1936 Hunger March was organised, naturally in conjunction with the national headquarters. London was really responsible for it but the local people in Aberdeen organised the local contingent.

Jim McCartney: Abject poverty. That's what took me in to the trade union movement, that's the answer, it was definitely abject poverty, I was the son of a fisherman.

David: Where did you stay ?

Jim McC: Right in the East End you couldn't be goin' further to the east in the city no matter where you lived. An ma father wis a fisherman a very affectionate man, but a very boozy man, drunken man. A big family, eight o' us. Mither had t' work hard to keep things together so that took me into the movement.

David: Tell me more about the poverty that you were trying to come out of.

Jim McC: Well, ma father an' mither, eight o' a family, there were two who died y'know. We lived in a 'butt an' ben'. Y'know, two rooms, an' as I said, my father was a very loving father but he couldn't get enough drink. He'd be coming home from sea an' he'd his money up here to give to my mither but he'd past about twenty pubs on the way home an' there wis always another ten bob comin' out an a five bob comin' out till well you know, I was brought up in that environment. I had to go down t' the fish market when I was nine, ten, to steal fish but it wasna stealin' it was lyin' there an' y'took it an' the bobby kent, an' the mate o' the boat that was in the quay, he knew it. He knew the unemployment, of course they did, an' I wasna the only laddie there.

David: A quarter of Aberdeen lived off the floor of the fish market.

Jim McC: Oh, yes.

Archie Lennox: Later efter the First World War, and this was before the (fish) sales, to prevent what we called 'chorin'. There was a break in the workin' day at that time an' people were coming' from that side of the town to this side of it and that was hundreds into thousands, and they carried a sweat rag with them! And everybody filled their sweat rags, and helped themselves out the boxes and of course if y' didna do that you knew a trawler man in the street like Jim's father he had a pilla slip o' fish for the neighbours.

Jim McC: You know a pillow slip, a pillow case, well it wis a blue check they all had blue check ones, that wis the custom. An that thing wis full o' fish and all the neighbours got. That wis oor job t' get fish for all the neighbours. We got an hapenny an' a penny y'know. You didna tell your mither that you got a hapenny or a penny off the neighbour. Maybe, you'd give her eight haddocks, filleted, clean fresh an you'd a penny. My father used t' supply his immediate neighbours.

Vera Hunter: I was born durin the war, my Granda was er like a spiv he was aye on the black market, deserted mair times than he wis awa, he wis in the navy really, an' er wallpaper at 'at time wis very difficult t' get but he'd got a few rolls o' wallpaper in an' he done up ma grannies hoose. The wifee doon the stair wis aye watchin' so she reported ma Granda t' the social, y' called it the 'U.A.B'. at 'at time that's fit y' caed it. An he got teen up foret, and up until the day he died he refused t' pay the fine so he did prison. He used t' do two days prison an' up until the day he died jist efter the war he made up his mind he'd pay the fine. Every time he wis unemployed which was very seldom he got a shillin' teen aff his unemployment benefit t' pay es fine. An' he wis still payin' it fen I wis sixteen years auld, an' I wasna born until 1942. He'd rather go t' prison than pay the fine.

THE PAWN

Ina Mackintosh: Lots of standards slipped after the war. People were still wearing mourning clothes after the war, folks would have put themselves in debt to get a black hat for a funeral. (interjection-that's why the pawnshops thrived!) I know that some of the Don Street folk.. but we didn't associate with them! (laughter) Some of them were real rough kind and they would put their suits in on Monday, and take them out on Saturday.

Mrs C Gimmingham: Where was the nearest pawnshop, was it in Loch Street?

George Simpson: If ye lost a pawn-ticket ye had to go in front of the J.P. and swear that ye niver sold it! It was the poor man's bank! The rich man could put his hoose up as collateral, but the poor man only had his suit.

> *"The rich man could put up his house as collateral, but the poor man only had his suit."*

William Simpson: The wife would take the suit in on Monday morning and get half-a-crown or five-bob, and she would probably have to pay 2/9 to get it back on the Saturday. The prices were the same at every pawn shop.

George: Celtic Andy, he was one of the very poor, and he never worked until he had to. He used to go to Auld Mill and chop up fire wood and things like that to get his money.

Jim Milne: Old Mill is now 'Glenburn Wing' at the front of Woodend Hospital but in those days it was one of the old Poor Law hospitals for down and outs. My father worked there and he, being from Frederick Street, knew most of the East End characters who ended up there. Talking about pawnshops, commonly called 'uncles'. It was not unknown for people to pawn their false teeth, take them out at the weekend (from the pawn) and put them back in on Monday!

Ina: Anybody who was unemployed didn't automatically get their giro, or whatever. They had to do something for it. In those days we used to get real snowfalls, and you'd be trudgin' through four or five feet of snow. There'd be queues of men at the Labour Exchange fightin' to get a shovel to clear the snow. They got 10d (4p) an hour. Those who wanted to work were desperate.

THE TICK MANNIE

David: What would families have to take out 'tick' on? (Tick was a form of credit.)

Man: O, onything they could get, food if it was possible. Clothes for the kids, household essentials.

John Londragan: But the bad thing about Sloan an' Co. was it was money that was involved, ye got money from them, nae goods, an' ye had tae pay back the money plus interest, an' if ye didnae pay the money, ye had tae pay the interest, and it was all added on. That was Sloan an' Company, still in George Street as a matter o' fact.

David: When would people go and borrow money from them?

John: It was usually on a weekly basis, most things were on a weekly basis. Pay was weekly for most people.

Man: For example there was a lot of East End people, you'd maybe get one who would form a weekly club. They'd maybe have 20 customers payin' a shillin' a week, which allowed them so much goods at £1 a week. But that was very, very odd, most times it was the Tickman.

John: Most of the clubs on the go, it wasn't even a shillin', it was a penny. A penny a week they paid, and this was mostly up till Christmas. And they could buy things then for Christmas. It was usually a neighbour would collect all the money every week. She wouldn't pay onything herself, but she would be counted as a club member.

David: So there would be a credit organisation set up by the people themselves. (Known as 'The Manager')

Man: That still goes on today in certain parts, you'll see big firms advertisin' house parties, for women's lingerie. At that time it was on a different basis. Credit was very rare, there was a proudness about the workin' class o' Aberdeen which is even passed on to this day. Pre-war, in my own home, I was very fortunate, my father was always in work in the granite trade. We were lucky in that m' mither never needed credit. M' mither and faither both were from big families, and it was very common for m' uncle tae come tae m' mither durin' the week and borrow a shillin' or maybe twa shillin's. It was always repaid, and there was nae interest charged.

Jim Milne: The Provident Clothing Co. Ltd., which is still trading, was known as the 'Provie'. The basis of the 'Provie' was to give low security loans, not cash but credit at certain shops who took the 'Provie' Cheque'.

> *"There was a proudness about the workin' class o' Aberdeen which is even passed on to this day."*

THE SOUP KITCHEN

Man: I'll tell you a funny thing aboot the workin' class people of that time.., there was a soup kitchen in Old Aberdeen, and it wis amazin' then how few people went to the soup kitchen. It was their pride, whether they were actually goin' hungry I couldn't tell you. There was very few who went up there with a pot or a pan for a fill-up. In West North Street there was what they called the Trust, and ye'd go up there to get a feed in the Hall, and ye'd see kids there queuein' wi' bare feet. That was about 1930, aye, they be queuein' wi' bare feet tae get a bit o' breakfast.

John Londragan: They used to put on religious festivals there every Sunday, an' all the children were invited along and they got a cup o' tea, an orange or an apple. This was every Sunday, but durin' the week they used to distribute bread and mugs o' tea and so forth. Down the street from there, next to Kelbie's rag store, there was a little wee place, a charitable organisation run by three women, they bought the second-days bread from the baker, practically got it for nothin' an' they used to distribute this on a charitable basis, these were the ladies from the West End. Down here slummin', I don't mean that badly, it was just that they were out of their element.

> *"they'd be queuein' wi' bare feet tae get a bit o' breakfast"*

Even the men in that area were gettin' up in the mornin' to go til their work, would go down there and get a cup o' coffee and a baked roll before they started their work for they didn't even get breakfast at home, it was that bad.

David: Would they do something similar at the Salvation Army Citadel?

John: The Salvation Army Citadel up here was commercial, it's always been commercial. They have a second-hand furniture store down there, household goods. They get everything for nothin', it's all gifted, but it's just not given away by them. There are teas an' that given away by the Salvation Army, but ye have tae go inside, sit down and take part in a religious ceremony. But what we were talkin' aboot was the soup kitchens, naebody ever questioned whit ye were, whit ye believed in or who ye were, just that ye were hungry. Then ye got yer bowl o' soup, cup o' coffee or whitever.

Man: I would say that the Aberdeen soup kitchens were very poorly supported considerin' the number o' workin'-class people that lived within a couple a hundred yards o' it, and originated in the East End.

HEALTH AND THE POOR

Jimmie Reid: Anither thing aboot these times, persons bein' ill or anything like that, at that time they would phone for the doctor, and the doctor would be there in a very short time. For that visit he used to charge you 2/6 (12p). Say during a period of three or four weeks, the doctor made 3 or 4 calls, maybe the person would have a bill for 10 shillin's for those calls, or 12/6 for five calls, a lot o' money, and you'd empty yer pockets, and the doctor would maybe throw in a call for 1/6 instead of 2/6. It would be a very unusual doctor in the East End if he didna give ye a bit back for he knew the sacrifices that was made tae get the ten shillin's t'gither.

> *" I'm not sure how I got T.B., but it was in the family and my eldest brother died of it"*

John Londragan: There was a doctor and his wife and they had a practice in King Street. He was called the poor people's doctor, he had sympathy with them, but they had tae pay, sometimes they paid on the spot, sometimes the bill would be sent til them. He knew all the families intimately and I know of a family that lived in the same hoose as me, an' he used to go there and he would take in pies tae them! The price of the pies was the price of the visit. Ye'd heard of the doctors in the country being paid with a rabbit or something, well the same thing happened in Aberdeen only in reverse, the Doctors would take food tae the patients.

   The doctors didn't get paid by the Government at that time, they lived on the subscriptions that they got from the patients. The only doctors that made any money were those that were consultants.

Jim: That Doctor that John wis talkin' aboot wis m' mither's doctor. Mither's family consisted of six brothers, two sisters an' grandfather an' grandmother. Dr. Moncur was the family doctor.

Bill Tinto: I was ill with Tuberculosis of both lungs and so I never worked until I was 25, apart from silly little jobs like message-boy. I worked in the town first in the transport department, then in the gas department, and then I left the gas department and went in for teaching under the special recruitment scheme. I took an Honours degree in English at the University and I went into teaching and I was there until I retired. I was teaching from 1962 until 1980. I taught first at the Old Academy, and then at the Grammar School. I worked for the Corporation from 1951 until 1958. I was working there when the gas department was nationalised. When I had TB I used to spend my time roaming about the country-side I was a keen naturalist. I'd go along the Kincardine Cliffs, up the Bullars of Buchan, through the nature reserves. I spent a lot of time outdoors, and that was what enabled me to get rid of it (TB).

   I'm not sure how I got TB, but it was in the family, and my oldest brother he died of it. I was about 16 when I got it.

   I never felt really ill with it, but when my brother who was very ill began spittin' up blood, the doctor sent me to the City Hospital. I had X-Rays, and I remember Dr. Banks showing me the marks on the lung. The last time I saw him he said to me "Many a man would give a thousand pounds to have a pair of lungs like these".

John Londragan: In the 1920's-30's the whole country, not just Aberdeen was riven with Rickets and Tuberculosis. These were the two big dangers especially for children. The Medical Officer of Health at that time, made the most foolish statement to parents, at a meeting at the Middle School, he told them that the only thing he could suggest was that they send their children to Switzerland and he was speakin' to people who couldn't afford to pay their rent!

Jim Milne: Overcrowding and poor nutrition were the main factors involved in contracting tuberculosis. T.B. sanatoriums were one of the few therapies available then but 1927 saw the opening of the new 'Special Unit' for T.B. patients at Woodend Hospital under local authority control.

THE MEANS TEST

From 1933 the relief received by the poor was assessed by using a means test which evaluated furnished rooms or sublets as income. In 1935 the scale was amended where only half the valuation of any furnished rooms was treated as income whilst in 1937 a distinction was made between "able-bodied unemployed" and the "ordinary poor" who were the old, infirm and disabled. The National Assistance Act of 1948 saw the end of local authorities providing social security.

* The scales of assistance appear on page 116

The Means Test

In the 1930's the 'means test' was one of the most despised institutions imposed on the working classes. People with low incomes and under the threat of unemployment lived in dread of having all their possessions assessed and, ultimately, removed before any government assistance was offered to them and their families. It was one of the causes of the so-called Hunger March in 1934.

Newspaper cutting heralds the setting up of the Unemployment Assistance Board

Jim Reid stated that when his parents were forced to undertake the means test, Sheriff Officers went through everything in his home marking the piano, gramophone, all his father's canes and all his mother's jewellery (with the exception of her wedding ring) for disposal before they would be granted any social security money. Often, however, the regulations didn't stop with the sale of 'non-essential' items (a term which could include plates or chairs in a household beyond the family's number), it could lead to families themselves being split up as the income of children and working wives was deducted from the eventual payments. This would force them to live elsewhere in order to protect their families and own quality of life. Worse things followed if people were obliged to live in the poor house because they were then segregated by sex and age, with whole families being divided up accordingly.

'When the Means Test Mannie came to inspect my Grandparents house he asked if there were any changes in family circumstances. My grandfather replied, "Aye the cats had kittens !" The Mannies were despised.'

Archie Lennox: I remember the means test commin' aboot and the unemployed workers movement was organised and be that time they were more interested in the social side among the leaders. It didna matter what the Communist Party did or said they were gettin' brushed aside so it was "All out boys, the means test is startin' in the mornin an we've got t' go on the streets." And I remember hearin' the commotion in the streets. They were paid somewhere af Guild Street because they had been separated fae the Labour Exchange they wer'nt the unemployed they were well divided then, them that were on benefit an' them that were on the means test. They used t' line up for the parish council benefit and you'd a got a queue, an' the archway along Union Terrace come in very handy. Aberdeen's thousands were all lined up underneath there. That was an important division that was created in the workin' class an' fen it came t' the General Strike commin' back t' that again, they were obeyin' what the union instructed.

Bill Morrice: My brother worked wi a cabinet maker, ken. At that time, like now, there wis a lot o' them jist finished and then he wis put on the means test, which meant, ma sister wis workin an' I was workin' and of course he wis telt, 'You'll get nothin'. So he sez 'I'm goin' I'm nae goin' t' bide here, I'm goin t' get digs or somethin', y'ken. That's the situation there was in families, he felt he was bein' kept by his breather and his sister, ken. Of course this was nae only my family - there wis huge demonstrations aboot it because the family income only came to a certain amount.

Jimmy Reid: I'll g'ye an idea o' the means test. My sister wis older than I was. The mother, father got their allowance but you got naethin' for the first child. What the mother and father received as an allowance had to carry the first child. When I was born an' brought up I was the second child. They got two shillin's a week that's ten pence a week for your second child. Now how the hell could anybody bring up a child on ten pence a week, it was ridiculous. That was the sort o' thing that was implanted in my mind.

David: What would two shillings buy in those days ?

————: Four pints o' beer.

————: Two shillin's, what would y' be, a dozen eggs ?

Bill Morrice: It was ruthlessly operated, I' mean there wis nane o' this humanitarian outlook. Some o' the families were in a state o' sheer desperation and the conditions they were livin' in were absolute slums. We were considered well off in Cotton Street because we'd a sink inside! The attic folk were the ones who got left oota this, they never got a sink inside an' there was one toilet, an ootside toilet for six families and the average family bein' aboot five or six. You could imagine at the week end an' the

Rosemount Viaduct from Jack's Brae

Tenement 'privie' with the kid's comics being put to good use!

queue on a Sunday mornin'! Fen I look back at the work ma mither had t' de, she wis jist a slave, a bloody slave. She got a job when ma father died, I was five at the time, she got a job cleanin' Commerce Street School an' then some o' her friends who were in the fishin' industry got her a job to learn t' mak nets. So, she cleaned the school, an' then she was able t' mak nets at hame, jist a blummin slave that's a' she was.

And this happened wi all workin' class families at that time.

Archie Lennox: That division in the workin' class, an' the means test. Before that they gradually got it by givin' you 'gap' periods. I landed in a gap period an' I was jist an apprentice. You turned up and all your benefits had been stopped. Now they give you no reason, you'd to except a gap period, it was most difficult. Now the N.U.W.M. was commin' to existence at this time. The National Unemployed Workers Movement and they dealt with cases where you had gap periods. Then they dealt with cases concerning the means test and that's where they functioned and became established.

Jimmy Reid: As a bairn I had the luxury of ma father workin'. But once he lost his job that was him finished because his war wounds stopped him working as a labourer or in industry. And seein' the means test bein' introduced where people were comin' into yer hoose an as a bairn watchin' this taken out and the next thing gettin' taken out before you could get ony money from the means test. I was only a kid at the time and it made an impression on me - if this is society, then I'll have to do something aboot it. That introduced me, comin' from, aye, gettin' nurtured by your people and parish an' gettin' parish boots. I'm a tall thin chap, an' t' pit on short troosers an' great big parish boots, I looked like one o' those chaps in one o' Lowery's paintings - a matchstick man!

Man: We originally stayed in Frederick Street. There was six o' us in one room there, with a wooden bed under the iron bed. The oldest brother, I and the brother after us, we slept in the wooden bed, and the youngest brother, he slept with the mother and father in the iron bed. In 1931/32 we obtained a house in School Avenue which consisted of a bedroom, a livingroom, a kitchen and a bathroom. Father and mother used the bed in what would have been the sittin'room, and we were thrown into the bedroom. But as I say, we were very lucky and never went hungry. It was workin' class economics, our mother managed quite comfortably an' we were very fortunate in so far as we never had to apply for school clothin' or boots or things like that. That was the biggest bugbear, school clothin'. For example, noo a child maybe goin' up to the Parish which was the equivalent of social security. Noo the first thing they did was tae advertise the individual's poverty for the boots they give them there was three holes placed in them on the uppers so that everybody knew it was 'school boots'. An' kids would make remarks about them.

Part Two

The Political Scene

THE HUNGER MARCH
was a response to poverty and unemployment and in particular to the Means Test.

This contribution by John Lennox is a truncated version of his original which is available in the publication entitled 'Voices From The Hunger Marches' Vol. 1. by Ian Macdougal.

John Lennox: While we had the longest and best organised march - it was over 700 miles from Aberdeen (to London) - we got the least publicity because it clashed wi' the Jarrow march. They had official backin': the corporation was behind them, the whole Labour movement was behind them. And they got issued wi' capes, groundsheets, ex-army surplus from the '14-'18 war. We didnae have that, we'd no ground sheets or nothin' like that. We were comin' doon the centre o' the country. The Jarrow march was doon there direct to London. Now they did 250 mile. But they got tremendous publicity: the Movietone News, the Gaumont Newsreel, all followed the Jarrow March. Ours didnae have the official backin'. It was organised by the N.U.W.M., Wal Hannington, Harry Pollitt, and they were Communists - in other words, it was communist inspired. That was the interpretation placed on it. (And that was why the media, the T.U.C. and the official Labour Party shunned it.)

The Aberdeen contingent had a banner. It said, 'Aberdeen to London. United against the means test.' It was carried all the time

Local press coverage of the Hunger Marchers as they set off on the trek from Aberdeen to Edinburgh - 1932

except if we were out in the country and out o' contact wi' the general public, then the banner was rolled up. What was lacking at first was music. The nearest approach we got to that was a kazoo, a toy submarine sort of thing that you hummed into. Oh, a' forget just where it would have been when we started getting these things but anyway we had this kazoo band and that helped a lot. And then it must have been in Fife or somewhere thereabouts miners came in and formed a kind o' Fife band.

So there was all kinds o' appeals went out to the trade unions. You've got to remember the background: in the official Labour movement the Citrines (After Lord Alfred Citrine who wrote a book on chairing meetings) and all these were in control, the right wing. The Hunger March, because it was organised by the N.U.W.M., was taboo officially. But there was tremendous sympathy and understandin' on the part o' the workers because they were livin' through the depression. They were all affected. If you were in a job you had a tremendous advantage: a grocer in the Co-op - 38/- a week (£1.90). A painter I knew in the Co-op he had two pound a week. He was

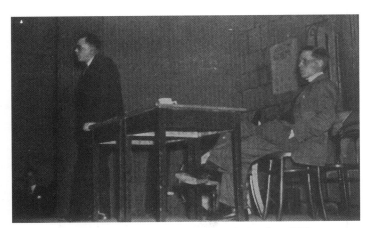

Top: Aberdeen Hunger Marchers en route to London - 1936
Bottom: Wal Hannington addressing a meeting in the Plaza, Prince Regent Street, on the night of the riot of 1934.

runnin' an Austin car, petrol was only 1/6d or 1/4d (7.5p or 6.6p) a gallon. At the same time you were affected by the unemployed because it was awfu' depressin'. People were people. Ye see, it's difficult to understand but people werena dressed. Ye found the backside was really hangin' oota your trousers at times. That wis the sort o' the conditions ye were livin' under. How I got involved in the Hunger March was, I come up as I say in 1935 to Aberdeen from London and I was engaged in politics. The proposed Hunger March was discussed for quite a while by the branch of the Scottish Painter's Society of which I was an active member. So it was agreed and I was elected to go on the march. I was the official representative of the Aberdeen painters' branch. Tom Rennie and myself were the only two marchers officially from a trades union.

We had set up the local march committee and it was seekin' funds and support. If I remember correctly we got fifteen blankets, lovely black velour blankets, from Grandholm Mills. Ye cannae beat Grandholm cloth. But that was the only provision we really got in the way o' equipment. We got instructions about what to take with us on the march and I've still got the paper. It said, 'suitable boots, overcoat, army valise, blanket, change of underclothing, plate, mug, knife, fork, spoon, shaving kit, towel, soap,' etc. But we jist wore what we had, wer ordinary clothes. Now other fellows some o' them had a bit o' an auld raincoat, well, probably from a jumble sale or the Castlegate or somewhere. There's no use o' sayin' they had their best clothes on, their working clothes or any thing else - jist the clothes they had.

When I heard I was to go on the march I bought myself a new pair o' boots. I thought I'd better do a bit o' practice for the march so I walked t' Dyce and back, a round trip o' twelve miles. When I come back I had blisters on my feet. So I had an advantage or an handicap: I started off on the Hunger March with blisters!

The 1936 march actually started in Aberdeen. There wis one representative from Inverness and one - Kensitt - from Peterhead. But they come and joined us in Aberdeen. There was about thirty two o' us set off from Aberdeen. The march set off from the Gallowgate. It was the 26th of September. And we had, oh, hundreds, thousands really - the whole streets were lined. And then of course the marchers were called to come into line. And I remember I looked round, I was watchin', just weighin' up this an that, an I say tae mysel', "Jesus, I'm bloody sure that half of us'll never make the Brig O' Dee." I didnae give much for my own chances because o' my experiences wi my boots tae Dyce! They were willin' but, oh, no, no there wis fellas physically caved in after years o' unemployment. They never had been nourished. Yet I would have to eat my words because it was hard to believe but the majority of them made it to London. So we set off and we were accompanied by the local people right to the Brig O' Dee.

The first overnight stop was Stonehaven where they found no reception and had to settle for the night in a hut down at the harbour sleeping on the floor without mattresses and only their Grandholm blankets for warmth.
The reception at Montrose was quite good with a reception committee whose efforts were linked with the churches in the district.

John: Ye see there was a human element whereever we went we created an awful stir. There was an emotional upsurge. People were sympathetic and responded.

A meeting was held in Montrose as in other towns and cities with the slogan 'Yer struggle's the same and it can be won, Organise, Mobilise, Join Up!' The next day they marched to Arbroath and the day after to Dundee.

John: Oh, but the reception in Dundee! Every town ye approached ye'd an army of two or three hundred really, och, even more than that. And Dundee, especially Dundee, was tremendous. It's a terrific boost to your morale. I addressed a meetin' in the city square at night. It wis jist absolutely a mass o' people, a kind o' miniature version o' when ye see the Pope in Rome speakin' to the crowds.

The march made its way south through Methil, Cowdenbeath and Kirkcaldy where they were received by the mining communities with a generosity and comradeship peculiar to miners and was to be found later when the march proceeded through Yorkshire and other mining communities. However things were different in Edinburgh.

John: We marched on then tae Edinburgh, across the Forth on the ferry. I'm sorry to say it but Edinburgh - oh, thon was the worst of all the places we were in! It was a Tory dominated place and it was a cold, cold reception we got officially from Edinburgh. I'm sayin' cold but maybe you could say it was a hot reception: the police were interferin' and guidin' us and directin' us and handlin' us and shovin' us here and shovin' us there.

Although the official response was poor there was a good response from those sympathetic to the cause.

John: We had a big meetin' in the Usher Hall, absolutely packed. And then we had meetin's on the Mound. The local comrades were really good, they tried their best.

From Edinburgh with about 200 marchers they proceeded to Gorbridge where they had a very cold night and from there to Galashiels.
The long distances covered by the marchers at this point were through sparsely populated areas resulting in few collections and very little food.

John: We were really hungry. As a matter of fact we had to send oot an appeal to the country. Supplies run oot a'thegither. We were the best part o' seven or eight days on that particular route before we got back into habitation.

Jock Winton was an official collector. We walked 750 miles thereaboot tae London but Jock must have done another 300 besides because he'd a' these other journeys. You would see a farm house right away over there, a mile there and a mile back again. And Jock would come back with a bloody hen. Now he swore blind that he was given it. He never come back empty handed, and he's rattlin' his collectin' box.

When we crossed the Border, well, of course being Scots they made the most o' the actual crossing - a conquering army come across wi' the banners wavin'!

The response o' the public was very good. They were sympathetic and concerned right enough. But right through from Galashiels tae Hawick tae Langholm, Carlisle, Alston, Middleton-in-Teesdale, Barnard Castle, Richmond - oh, that was a real Tory place, Richmond - Rippon and Harrowgate, right until we reached Leeds - oh, no, no, no!

And by gosh it was a wonderful reception in Leeds. We caused tremendous stir. It made you feel awful important like, a' the people that was interested. They gave us clothes - the boys were a' getting new trousers: after all, their boots and their claes wis, well, they were sleepin' in them, walkin' in them. So we got dressed in Leeds. Leeds was the one place that really made a tremendous difference.

From Wakefield through the mining area of Barnsley where the reception was both encouraging and welcoming, the march continued through Rotherham and Sheffield and on to Chesterfield.

John: They told us it was market day in Chesterfield but that we werenae goin' tae be permitted to go through the High Street where the market was held. Well, it was put to the marchers and the marchers decided that they were goin' to go through. By this time there would be 200-odd on the March. So we formed up and jist marched in. Right across the road was about fifty policemen, a double row o' them. so we jist ppphhhcchh - jist swept the police aside. That was a real victory for us.

Eventually, the Scottish East March and the Scottish West March joined just North of St. Albans.

John: Oh, it was a tremendous sight. Peter Kerrigan was leadin' the West, Harry McShane and Alex Moffat were leadin' the East. We must ha' been about 800 strong or probably nearer a thousand I should imagine. It's a sight you would never forget.

The final place was Willesden. This was the sort o' assembly point for the final march into London. And because we had been the longest on the road the East o' Scotland got the honour o' leadin' the March in to London.

The reception they got was tremendous both on their journey and at Hyde Park where there were various demonstrations.

John: I was on the platform with Sir Stafford Cripps and S.O.Davies. This was an official Labour Party rally in support o' the March and I was delegated to go as a guest speaker. I was jist to make a ten minute contribution. But, oh, the reception! I had never experienced anything like it before.

The Hunger March was one o' the highlights of my life really. There was conviction behind it, ye see. There was real purpose, we did gain. There was changes in the means test and there was concessions the Government did make as a result o' the march.

THE MORNING AFTER.—The crowd in Castle Street this forenoon discussing last night's riot.
("Evening Express" copyr.

POLITICAL ACTIVISTS

'Riotous scenes at the Castlegate'

John Lennox: In Aberdeen we were the first ward to return a Labour councillor about 1920, George Catto. The Lennoxes were all engaged in that campaign.

After I left school, when I was about fifteen or sixteen I joined the Independent Labour Party Guild o' Youth. I was in that for a wee while. The I.L.P. was a strong propaganda force. It was up and doon the whole o' Scotland. Aberdeen was no exception and there was quite a strong branch here. As a boy I used to sell the 'Labour Leader', 'New Leader', and Tom Johnston's paper 'Forward'. Bob Cooney, a Communist Party activist, who was a year younger than me, he'd be sellin' 'The Workers Weekly' or some o' these papers. We had a cinema on Sunday evening where we held this meetin's and on a winter's night we would be inside and we did allow Bob to stand in the doorway if it was really wet. But we kept him at arms length. Well, in Aberdeen the Communist Party did eventually come tae be capable o' gettin' meetin's. But at that time in the 1920's they werena the propaganda force the I.L.P. were locally.

Top left: A crowd gathers in Castle Street on the morning after the riot
Top right and Above: Press coverage of the events
Left: A policeman strikes out at the raised fists of a Communist rioter

"Riotous scenes at the Castlegate and the 'Plaza' in Prince Regent Street last night had sequel in the Aberdeen Police Court today when four young men appeared before Bailie McKay in connection with charges of having formed part of a disorderly crowd and breach of peace. Three also charged with assault on police. David May, Baker, 47 Green, George Hamilton, railway gateman, 4 Cotton Street, John Londragan, Carter, 117 West North Street, Albert Gow, no occupation, c/o 12 Marischal Street. Police had to baton charge to disperse over 200 men in Castle Street who marched to Prince Regent Street and again police charged the same mob at the 'Plaza' where a meeting of the N.U.W.M. was being held."

Newspaper coverage of the trial and convictions following the riot

David: John, who were you representing when you were helping to rehouse the evicted folk?

John Londragan: At that time I was a member of the Communist Party but politically we didn't use the Communist Party regarding this particular activity. We set up a committee for rehousin' people ourselves, do you understand, a committee it was done by. There were people in the Communist Party and any other party for that matter, it was an effort by the people themselves. I will admit that like myself, members o' the Communist Party took a leadin' part in it.

David: Who were the Communist speakers in the Music Hall around that time?

John L: Bob Cooney, finest o' the lot, er Davie Campbell, Tom Baxter, he was a councillor for Footdee. We had plenty o' good speakers an' good organisers an that y'know.

David: They spoke in Justice Street and the Music Hall....

John L: The Castlegate was a favourite spot, every Sunday. Sometimes we'd be there at four o'clock in the mornin', Monday mornin' goin' hame havin' something to eat change my clothes and away to my work. No sleep or anything. I never thought nothing of it, except its part of the way of life at that particular time.

John Lennox: By that time I was a member of the Communist Party. I joined it in London in 1928 in the Wandsworth Road. While I was in London and comin' back and forth to Aberdeen I'd quite a lot o' association with Bob Cooney. So when I came back in 1935 we sort o' picked up where we left off. In Aberdeen the Communist Party met in what you called the 'All Power Hall'. The locals called it the 'All Power Hallie'. It's still there in Loch Street, an old buildin', dilapidated. It had an old rickety stair. Of course they did their best to paint it up and make it as attractive as possible. The ceiling was likely to collapse at any time so there was a beam supporting it. And on this beam was the slogan, "All Power to the Workers!" It was really funny. So that was the All Power Hallie. Bob Cooney and his brother George used to perform on all the social occasions. It wasnae jist party members, the public come in an' a'. So Bob and George used to do sketches and things and took opportunity to put across propaganda.

THE FASCISTS

A Fascist speaks in the Castlegate - 1934

Archie: Now a while afore the Castlegate was the debatin' chamber o' Aberdeen's problems, you had Basil Taylor an' some others, their names have gone outa my head at the moment but they were the Anti Parliamentarian Communist League — everybody lived only a stones throw away from the Castlegate an' the word went around, once it started, the Fascists they started t' have meetin's, they never had a proper meetin' in Aberdeen —

Jim McCartney: Chambers Hunter, he was the local Fascist.

David: Were you around when Mosley came to speak ?

Jim and Archie: Aye

Archie: He said that he would be back and he hired a steam wagon and the police were gettin' tired to a certain extent and they put him up to—

Jim: South esplanade east.

Archie: And most o' that area was a coal yard and he was located there -

Jim: But that wasna Mosley, Archie, that was Chambers Hunter he was a laird, he'd an estate over at -

Archie: Within aboot ten minutes there was about thirty tons o' coal, we were all throwin' coal at him an so, that was toot! toot! the driver toot! toot! an' away. But the very last one was the Austin car with a sunshine roof an' Chambers Hunter with his kilt on. His sister was there or his sister in law. An' she fell and on that occasion the crowd moved in an' before he knew where he wis, Chambers Hunter kilt an all up side doon.

Jim: Her clothes, she wis nobility y' know, an' her clothes went right ower her head an' there was a local wit there, he worked the shipyards, an' he, jist spontaneously he said, 'O Jeanies white drawers'(Laughter) (To the tune of Two lovely black eyes.) Everybody jined in y' know! An' that wis the finish o' Chambers Hunter in Aberdeen. There was a few skirmishes after that but that was the catalyst.

At that time we were the district committee, 'City committee' we called it we met on a Friday night. Each member would tek a pot o' white wash an' you'd do your usual (paint slogans) on your way home, you'd do your chalk up, either chalk or white wash. I remember that night well 'cause I stepped back into a pot o' white wash. (laughter) I was workin' on the railway at that time an' workin' shift work so I cam in at the last an' that was the daft thing that I did. It was ever so beautiful 'Fascists Out!' right along the dyke where the Denburn, from Union Terrace Gardens y' read it right along. An' y' seen it off the bridge. Mosely was in the Caledonian Hotel the police took a cordon on each end an' y' had to have a good reason to go past the police cordon so we did see him intae the winda occasionally 'cause we were near enough to even shout and that was the most we could see. The press didna do justice til us that week.

WOMEN

The suffrage movement fought from 1832 onwards to give women the vote. In Aberdeen, the cause was taken up by the Scottish Women's Liberal Movement. The headlines however were made by members of the Militant Woman's Social & Political Union none of which were Aberdonian but they came North to lead demonstrations, disrupt public meetings and organise publicity stunts. In 1912 this came to a climax with an attempt to set off explosive caps at a Liberal meeting in the Music Hall and an arson attack on Ashley Road School. The First World War forced the issue off the political agenda, but the key role of women during the war meant the government could not deny them the right to vote. The 1918 Representation Of The People Act limited the vote to propertied women over thirty. The franchise was then extended to women of 21 in 1928 and in 1929 Britain's first female MP was elected. The vote however did nothing to elevate the role of women or increase their wages. Married and single women went out to work or worked from home as an economic necessity. Some of the women in Aberdeen worked in heavy industry during the Second World War, others in factories, offices and shops. They encountered various working conditions, wages and attitudes but all of them have vivid memories of their time and experiences in the workplace.

John Lennox: I come from a family interested in politics. It was not my father it was my mother who was the driving force in our political activities. Even as a schoolboy I went with my mother on a Sunday night to a local cinema, when Davie Kirkwood, Jimmy Maxton, George Buchanan, Neil Maclean, Rev. Jimmy Barr come up and were speakers. And there was Gallacher and Saklatvala M.P. That was the sort of background we had.

My mother was a bit o' a suffragette. She wisnae actually in the suffragette movement but she had that tendency and always worked for women's freedom. She wasn't a feminist in the modern sense but she was keen on women's liberation. So it was her that introduced all the family to this political activity.

Man: My own doctor was Dr. Angus-Thompson who was a female doctor. Never a Christmas or a birthday passed but I always got somethin'. There was a teddy-bear that was in the hoose for years and years.

John Londragan: There was a lot of prejudice at that time, particularly as regards men and women doctors. They just wouldn't go in front of a woman doctor. They'd wait until the man was available. If he wasnae there they'd go away and come back again. The women doctors had a hard time breakin' intil the minds of the people, tae get trusted and so forth. With kids an' that it was all right, but it was the male population where the prejudice was.

Trevor: And what did the women do, stay at home or go to work?

John Londragan: Recht up until 1937 the only women that worked were the daughters that worked in the paper makin', the textile works and the fish in particular. Married women didna' work, their job was the house and that didn't change till the war started, when the men went away there was a shortage of staff for industry and they started recruitin' married women to come back into industry. Up until that point the married women stayed at home.

> *" ... it was my Mother who was the driving force in our political activities."*

LABOUR WINS -- ATTLEE PREMIER

MAJOR CLEMENT ATTLEE, who, as leader the Labour Party, now in pow has taken his place as Pr Minister of Great Britain, and this capacity has returned Potsdam to continue the Th Power Conference.

MR HECTOR HUGHES, K.C., who retained the North Aberdeen seat for the Labour Party with a large majority, is congratulated by his Union-

Local newspaper headline proclaiming the Labour Election victory of 1945

THE CHANGING SCENE :-

The Labour victory in 1945

During October 1994 Tony Benn was invited to open an exhibition in Aberdeen called, 'For the Rights of Labour' which was to commemorate the founding of the Trades Council in the city 125 years before.

Whilst in Aberdeen, Tony Benn and other members of the Trades Council got together informally to talk about various political topics. The extract below is not only politically enlightening but puts Aberdeen in context with the country at large.

David: What we want to know is how did the Labour Party manage to get that landslide win in 1945 and seem to have gone backwards since then ?

Tony Benn: Well it's a very interesting question and I'll tell you what I think and you tell me if I'm right. I think the ingredient in 1945 that tipped it was hope. We'd beaten Hitler, we'd beaten Mussolini and the people turned their backs on the 1930's with unemployment and the means test; they just turned their backs on it and said 'We'll build a new Britain', and the difference that I noticed, and you'll notice it more than me between young people, - when I was twenty in '45 I thought we could do anything. We could have full employment, we can build a welfare state, we can have a health service, we could have peace and in a way we did. Where as now young people have been beaten into the ground, there is nothing you can do if it isn't profitable, don't expect a job and so on. Until we can raise morale among the general public it is hard to make a change. It doesn't matter what the leaders do, 'cause after all Clem Attlee, whatever you might say about him, he wasn't exactly a very televisual figure. He was short, he was as bald as a coot, he had a little moustache and yet he beat Churchill. Why, 'cause people wanted a change, I mean, Attlee was a remarkable man, I'm not belittling him but he was not exactly what you might call a media star it was what happened to the people that changed it all ....

Archie Lennox: ..the anticipation for the welfare state particularly the propaganda from the Trades Council that was a great attraction t' people. Basic things.

Tony Benn: Somebody sent me a photograph the other day and I'm going to copy it for the next election. It was a poster and it said, 'Vote for Beveridge and Jenny Lee': D'you know - instead of voting Labour, vote for jobs, vote for houses, linking us to the issues rather than these awful glossy roses.

Archie: I think you'll agree with me that despite the rent controls that was bought in 1950/60's government were afraid t' tackle that question of a standard rent. Y' see the property o' the houses were gettin' older all the time, there were no rents bein' paid t' them for repairs those that were bein' squatted in particular an' the two parties which against an amendment. No, the standard rent was safe with us.

Jimmy Reid: As far as I'm concerned, my father was badly wounded in the First World War. He come back, he did get a job but during the depression he lost that job and seein' me as a bairn an' ma sisters on the means test, goin up t' the parish t' get boots on wi feet an' get stuff t' go t' school, it made an impression on me as a bairn - it'll never happen again.

I made my vote, I voted proxy because I was stationed away durin' the war and believe you me I did my damnedest to vote for the Labour Party.

Tony: They mainly did didn't they?

Jimmy R: They mainly did.

David: It's quite interesting the idea of the brave new world in '45, what made it go back in favour of the right wing?

Top: Tony Benn with Archie Lennox
Centre: ...with Councillor James Lamond
Bottom: ...in relaxed mood, James Dun's House.

Tony: I think there were a lot of factors, first of all there were a lot of shortages at the end of the war. We carried on rationing for six years, indeed we actually rationed bread for the first time after the war, we never really rationed during the war. People got fed up with it and people promised t' set the people free, but the most important factor was the cold war. We were told from 1946 till 1989 that the Red Army was going to invade us so that every socialist became criminalised as a K.G.B. agent spying for the Kremlin. The more I think about the cold war the more I think the whole thing was a trick to destroy the people's faith in socialism although our socialism would never have been what Stalin was up to but they used the word the same. There was never any intention by the Russians to invade the West but what they were afraid of was socialist ideals and when I look back, - I remember Aneurin Bevan's resignation speech in 1951 when Gaitskell introduced the budget you remember and put on a charge for teeth and spectacles. I think that I was right about that and he'd said that he didn't think that the Russians intended to invade us and he was right. I think that the cold war was the most awful thing that ever happened politically and the people stood up against it like Julian Hornes and then they called him a communist and anyone who wanted peace in Germany. Jim Mortimer, general secretary of the Labour Party later, he was expelled from the party, for why, because he was a member for the committee for peace. That's what I feel, I don't know whether other people agree but I think that is a very big factor in trying to turn people against socialist ideas.

David: Can you identify specific qualities of life before the war that were improved after the war by the trade union movement or the Labour Party?

Tony Benn: Well, it was the trades unions that set up the Labour Party and it was the Labour Party that set up the Welfare State and the National Health Service and it's an interesting point that, the most popular thing we ever, ever did was the most socialist thing that we ever, ever did ie., set up the health service based on health care according to need and not wealth. I've still got the leaflet issued in June 1948 saying on July the 1st all medical treatment, all surgical treatment, everything optical, dental treatment will be free. Now that's still the most popular thing so it wasn't that people turned against socialism - well I think that was its greatest achievement and full employment without any doubt did more to transform peoples lives than any other single factor. It opened up jobs for women, for young people, it allows all sorts of things and that's why they don't want full employment now they want to keep people down by unemployment, I think.

Harry Bygate: What amazes me nowadays is the young people, the unemployed are not organised. In the 1930's every workin' class group was organised and politicised. Now there's no political leanin' for them. As a life long member of the Labour Party I was never tempted to go further left than the Labour Party.

Tony: I think the 'clause four' thing is a terrible mistake. It means that the next twelve months will be Blair attacking our article of faith instead of the Tories. If he succeeds, which he might do, then it'll be 'what about the trade unions, what about' — I mean, once you throw your children to the wolves the wolves just go on following you. So I think that's a mistake. On the future for young people, it's about the system it's not about the Tories. I think we spend too much time about the Tories we should spend more time on the cause of it. While people believe that profit is the only criteria - of course there will be young people on the dole and the trouble is that we don't only not talk about socialism any more, we don't talk about capitalism any more. If you discuss capitalism that's considered unhelpful but it's capitalism we are living under and why can't we discuss the system? Why it works and how it works that's where we come back to your point comrade, the Communist Party was the university of socialism within the Labour movement and unfortunately it was never affiliated to the Labour Party for a variety of reasons. Firstly, they wouldn't come in and then Labour wouldn't have you in but you influenced the Trade Union Movement the Trade Union Movement influenced the Labour Party and with the disappearance of the Communist Party the Labour Party has become a sort of Fabian society if you know what I mean, floating about without any real understanding of the roots of its own faith. I don't remember socialism being talked about by our leadership since 1945. Attlee was a very good socialist but since then it's always been 'keep your head down keep your options open and don't rock the boat and you'll float in', and of course it's not very easy to float in. The S.W.P. (Socialist Worker's Part.) although I'm not a member of it, at least they're doing things on the streets. I yearn to see Labour posters saying 'Labour supports the Miners, Labour against the criminal justice bill.' They leave it to militant, to the S.W.P. and then wonder why the S.W.P. attract the young people. We should be attracting those very same people.

Part Three

At Work

Aberdeen folk's experience of work between
1925 and 1955.

THE GRANITE INDUSTRY

If there is one industry synonymous with Aberdeen it is granite. In 1764 the decision made in London to pave its streets with Aberdeenshire granite gave the initial impetus to the granite trade. By the end of the 19th century the quarrying of granite had expanded to such an extent that other local industries switched from making farm machinery to the manufacturing of machinery required for this hugely expanding industry. As time progressed the demand for a greater variety of granite saw Aberdeen importing stone from Scandinavia. By the beginning of the First World War there were over ninety firms in the granite industry with a work force of approximately two thousand. As far as the United Kingdom was concerned, the granite industry was virtually exclusive to Aberdeen. Nevertheless, in terms of numbers employed, other industries were far more important. In the 1920's for example, there were about 6,000 employed in the metal work industries, whilst only about 1,800 in granite. (See the 1921 census.) Since the beginning of the First World War the granite industry has slowly and irrevocably declined till only a few yards were left working in the 1950's. Currently (1996) there are only three granite manufacturers operating. Of the two main quarries, Rubislaw closed in 1970 with only Kemnay remaining open.

Gilbert Mackland: I started workin' in the granite when I left school when I was fourteen. I went to work for Gordon Graham's. I was there to serve my apprenticeship, I worked there for a year. What happened then was, the chap died, the boss died; his brother was left the business and it went bankrupt. Then my father was a mason and he said that it was a waste of time looking for a three year apprenticeship you'd get more as a first year mason. So I went and served my apprenticeship in a granite yard in Aberdeen in 1948. J.O.R. Rettie which was in Merkland Road. I served my apprenticeship there for two years, then I broke my apprenticeship to move to another granite yard. The wages were very poor in that days, I think that my apprenticeship was only aboot two pounds a week. Trainees, came into the trade, we called them 'Diluties'. It was a bit unfair for apprentices because an apprentice mighta been workin' for a firm for two years then a lad woulda come in oota the army an' he would go on to two thirds a journeyman's wage. So I left there to work for another granite firm to finish of my apprenticeship called J.M. Stocker in Jute Street. An' I stayed there till my apprenticeship was out then I moved on to there to do my National Service in the Army.

> *"His back was*
> *actually curved*
> *into the shape*
> *he worked in."*

David: What did your apprenticeship consist of ?

Bert: When I started at J.O.R. Retties first, we started in the mornin' at eight o'clock, we worked for five and a half days. Y' worked from eight till five, Monday t' Friday then Saturday mornin' from eight t' twelve. The first job y' started with was dressin' blocks of granite, preparin' blocks of granite. They come outa the granite supply an' y' dressed off a face. When you'd done that it went onto a 'Dunter'. This was a big old fashioned machine, it was an awfa dirty job, an' granite is jist like metal. Y' find you're gettin' cuts all over your hands a' over your face.

Woman: We used to walk along King Street an' you could see them all at lunch time; their lunch consisted of a flask o' tea and sandwiches, they never got out, but you would see somebody with all these little cuts like a drunk man had been shavin'. It wis the men hittin' the granite an' the chips flyin' up an' at that time they didna have safety goggles or safety gloves. If you was goin' along King Street an'

Top: Fitting 'feathers'
Bottom: Kemney Sett maker, working in his "scathie" (shed)

you seen somebody comin' you'd say, "Oh this is a bloke frae the granite yards", it was so obvious. With their hands and faces cut it must have been a very dangerous job with no protection for their eyes.

David: What Bill was tellin' me was, they did protect their eyes. What they used to do was find an old pair of spectacles take out the glass then they'd use the machinery for cutting squares of glass that fitted the glasses. Next they'd use their own tools and grind them down till they fitted the shape of the glasses and they'd wear those.

Woman: My father in law used t' speak about the dust. He polished an' the dust went doon into his chest. He died of a form o' leukaemia. *(Ed. This would probably be silicosis.)*

David: What, working in the granite?

Woman: Aye from the dust. A form o' cancer from the dust. And of course he wis in the First World War. He was in the trenches with the gas an' that then he cam back to his trade, then the dust an' arthing come off the stones. He wis only 62 when he died.

Bill: The duntin' machine was a machine that went up and doon. There was a big pick that sat in the centre of it full o' teeth, huge thing about that size, (sic) an' they were all sharpened by the blacksmith, what y' call firesharp. We used t' fit the granite in this machine and hold it wi a handle and y' went across the stone and it vibrated ower the top o' it an' that knocked a' the rough bits doon flat. Then it went into a polishin' machine and then it wis ground down flat by the abrasive, what y' called the Jenny Linn. And then it wis polished and then they used t' put it into the old fashioned swing saw and cut aff the head pieces for the gravestones. It wis all cut out o' this, big blocks, y' know. Then they went into the carborundum saw. (This wis before we had diamond saws.) This guy worked this auld fashioned carborundum saw and they pit em in doon flat an' cut em t' aul the sizes they needed. That's in the days when they used abrasives, what they used was like ball bearin's, what they called the 'Shotser' it worked with water. What they used t' do, they used t' get a big stick an' nail it to an old syrup tin. There was a big bath o' water at the bottom near where the saw made the cut, this was with the old pendulum saws and it would just grind along at a helluva noise. Well, y' fed these little balls of shot into the cut that the saw had made and then you fed it with water and they used this stick and syrup tin t' pick up the water an' feed the cut. That was a job that was given to laddies some of them couldna read or write and all the lads wi poor education they started on the old fashioned saw.

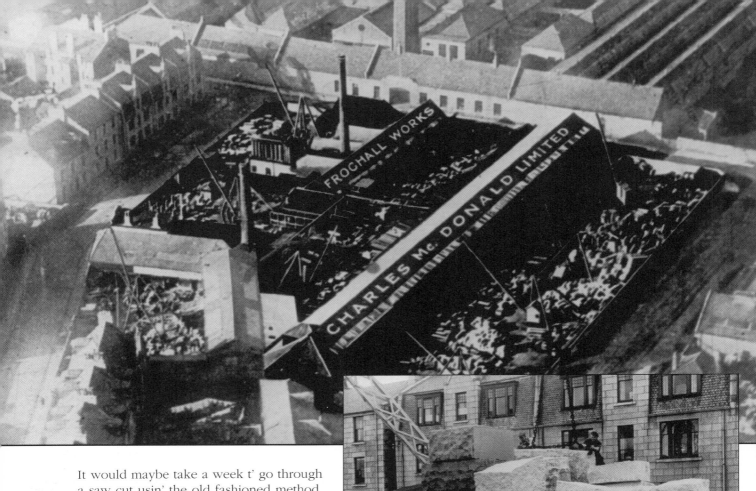

Top: Charles McDonald, Froghall Works - note the wooden jib cranes and tall lums (steam power)
Bottom: Stock yard - "Dogs" being fitted to "Dogholes" for lifting

It would maybe take a week t' go through a saw cut usin' the old fashioned method. Then it went from there to the mason's bunkers and they fashioned them into gravestones. Then it went into the old fashioned borer t' bore the container hole. That was done wi an old fashioned shot borer an' it used t' take aboot three hoors t' boor, now we can do it in two minutes. It's marvellous how it's changed. Of course, in that days labour was comparatively cheap an' y' got a lot o' men an' a lot o' apprentices which we don't have now.

David: Do you have any apprentices here now?

Bert: Oh, aye we've got one, two er four altogether.

David: I was told that craftsmen often studied the classical sculptures in the art gallery to obtain their designs. What is your knowledge of this.

Bert: Once you had cut an ornamentation on the stone y' took a piece o' paper an' put it across the carvin' then y' rubbed a piece o' crayon across the paper an' that took an imprint of what you've already done on the stone. Well you just put the number of the design on it an' y' put it in a filing cabinet so the next one y' did y' took oot the papers or whatever design was wanted glued it onto the stone, there was no need for a draughtsman unless there was onything new. The tradesmen did nearly arthing an' far they got a' their designs from originally have come off wallpaper samples!

Ernie Mundie: My father worked for the same granite company, Hoggs in Regent Walk.
   I was proud o' him, he was the top man in his trade, he was a stone-polisher, but he could do three trades. He got about 2d an hour more than the standard rate. If a special job come in, m' father would perhaps be selected for it, an' he would maybe get time and a quarter, so if he was gettin' one and six old money an hour, (7.5p), he'd maybe get one and ten (just over 9p). On top o' that, I've heard him tell

a story about the boss slippin' him an extra 10 bob (50p), the equivalent of an extra five hours work.

At one time all the one side of King Street was Granite works. All the way down to University Road, there was about eight or nine of them. From Mealmarket Street, all the way down.

Man: They used to import granite, Swedish...

Ernie M: Aye, but in earlier days it was all local granite, Rubislaw granite, Peterhead granite, the whole toon was based on it.

William Simpson: Oor faither wis in the granite trade, He wis with AA Brown in Advocates Road.

George Simpson: Aye, 52 year.

Bill: He wis a yard foreman for a lang time. He was a polisher tae trade, what they ca' a 'han' rubber', that's a hand-polisher cos' they did the bits at that time, that the machines couldnae dee.

George: O' coorse they had machines latterly, first they had air-machines and then electric drills which were converted.

Top: Polishing Mill, Jute Street - 1875
Bottom: Masons' covered yard at Charles McDonald Ltd. - 1921

David: Was there a granite place down Urquhart Road?

George: That was the Granite Supply, that was a wholesaler..

Bill: All the granite merchants owned that, well most of them anyway. And that's where all the imported granite went. If any of the yards wanted that stuff, that's where they went.

George: Quite a bit of the granite came from Aiberdeen itself.
But not in Urquhart Road. The granite came from Kemnay Quarry, Correnie, Rubislaw and Peterheid. That was the main ones.

Kemnay Quarry - 1879

Bill: Correnie quarry was ootside Banchory, Banchory's built oot of it. There's a sort o' pinkish-reid tinge in that granite.

There was one at Belhelvie, belonged to the County Cooncil, that was just road-metal. There was one just beyond Black Dog, that was sand only, and belonged to Johnson's. Then there was a quarry at Bucksburn, they used to make all the pavin' slabs.

There was a granite quarry in Old Aberdeen, there was one at Loanhead.

George: There was Croft's, that's where Robertson's granite works is now, there was Ruddiman's, there was Edwards', ...

Bill: At one time there was 38 yards in Aberdeen. These were mostly yards where monuments were made. They did stone-dressing and polishing and sculpture.

George: I worked in every granite yard in Aberdeen in my time. There were no diamond-saws then. The swing-saws were hard-metal blades, and they were cooled with white-shot and water. It was the shot that actually did the cuttin', and Gibbs in King Street, were the first to make multiple-blade saws. I've known up to 12 blades on a saw. It was a production-line. You could cut fine slabs for facing.

Bill: My father's last job was the Foundation Stone for John Knox's Kirk.

George: He did the Bank at the corner of St. Nicholas Street. Some of the granite was polished by what they called 'hand rubbin'. It was polished by hand, because the machines couldnae do it. Cassie invented the machine which was operated by compressed air. It was operated by an air drill which was actually made by the Consolidated Pneumatic Tool Company in Fraserburgh, and Cassie converted it intil a machine for hand-polishing. Later it had an electric motor fitted, and it was a much lighter machine to handle. They would drill holes for the letters and then pour in lead and cut them out with a knife. It was a very skilled craft the letter-cutters, then you had the carvers. They carved the Lions at the County Hall. That was carved by Jack Sinclair.

Bill: Kemnay is the nearest quarry to Aberdeen now. It was too costly to extract the granite. Rubislaw quarry is a quarter-mile deep!

There is a quarry at Peterhead. But it's not the part that the prisoners work in.

The prisoners who got hard labour worked in the quarry, and the prison-officer would stand over them. It was a long time till anybody escaped from Peterhead.

George: Remensky was the first one.

Bill: He was a Pole. He was caught at Ledingham's Bakery. He was a safe-blower.

Ernie Mundie: I started work at Clinterty t' serve ma time as a builder mason. And y' served for four years, two years in the quarry an' two years on the scaffold, supposed t' be. The first year wis spent dressin' stones for council houses. According to the rules at that time, it was two apprentices t' each trades man but it never worked like at in the two an' a half years I was there. Tradesmen builders didna like workin' in the quarry 'cause they had t' work — it was a sair job workin' bent over fa eight or nine hours a day. As a matter o' fact the foreman at the quarry was known as John Harry. He lived in Aul' Aberdeen an' he wis bent double. He'd done nothing since he left school but dressed stone and his back was actually curved in to the shape that he worked in. He actually walked like that bent double because all that he did all his life wis stan'in dressin' stone. You're supposed t' spend a year doin' that an' then y' progressed t' dressin' stones for winder sills, lintels, doorsteps an' stuff like at. For specialised granite y' used hand tools axes, an' picks an' you could be standin' a whole day doing nothing but axin' at a stone. All your axe cuts on the granite had t' be one way an' when it wis finished it wis actually smooth with jist wee cuts in the granite. If you g' roond some o' the old buildin's in Aberdeen yet y' can pick oot stones which were dressed in this manner.

David: Was it a specialist skill ?

A selection of postcards sent back from America by North East quarrymen working there during the Scottish winters

Ernie: It wis a part o' your trade, after y' spent y' second year dressin' stones y' got pit out t' the scaffold as we called it. Y' got put out on the buildin' site. Y' learned t' build walls, read plans and things like that.

The buildin' trade in the 30's was in a poor way. I worked for a good employer in Inverurie, he very seldom paid off his men in winter time. A buildin' mason in the winter was laid off possibly for four months. He was laid off nearly every winter for four months at the time o' the frost an' the snow because at that time y' couldna build hooses in frost. I've known a foreman mason build council houses in Inverurie, he built the same house three times actually because every time he built the house in the frost, when he went in the mornin' the walls were down because they jist collapsed.

David: So what did building workers do in the winter then?

Ernie: They signed the brew but my boss used t' pit them into the quarry t' dress stones. The quarry I worked in was this side o' Blackburn village called Clinterty an' that was as deep down as it could be before it started drawin' water. Once it started drawin' water you had t' start usin' pumps. The lack o' foresight in quarryin' at that time - this is hearsay that I'm sayin' now but they built their quarries in such a way that they built them narrow an' they went down an' once they got down so far, they started drawin' water but they couldna get out the way because everything they had taken out o' the bottom o' the quarry they tipped jist over the lip o' the circle so they couldna get down into the granite because they had tipped all the rubbish above the good granite so that most of the good quarries up here were wasted.

I joined the Territorials on the 1st o' May '39 and I was called up on the 1st o' September 1939 . I spent six and a half years on active service and I was demobbed on the 1st o' May 1946. I was given a class B release, where y' got a provisional discharge from the services to come back into your trade but y' didn't get your gratuity which was money paid by the government gave ye for spendin' y' youth and servin' yer country and after seven years I got eighty one pounds.

Speakin' aboot the granite industry before the Boer War in Kemnay quarry they were laid off for the winter and there was a man be the name o' Klerrihew? took the men abroad to America to a place called Vermont. He took them out there and they were there every winter. I had an uncle that went out there, - but they left their wives at home an' they cam home again an' worked in Kemnay quarry an' went back again. He sent home post cards to his family every so often. The stamps on the post card started at about 1902 and the postcards were still coming in to Kemnay in 1910. The boats came in with timber an' went out with immigrants.

Woman: My father's uncles' used t' do that, they were in the granite trade. They went t' Canada and they came back in the summer.

Ernie: He sent home these sentimental post cards y' see and he sent home photographs of the quarries and where he stayed in a hostel an' places like that.

The reason I didn't g' back into the buildin' trade was that I could see the shape o' things t' come. The granite trade at that time at the start o' the war was goin' down 'cause it was gettin' too expensive to extract, dressed and so after seenin' the situation down in England and abroad if you had your wits about y' ye could see the shape o' things to come and the granite trade as such was finished at that time even 'cause it was all gonna be bricks. Another thing that was on my mind was that at the age of twenty five I couldn't afford t' be idle for four months of the year.

THE FISHING INDUSTRY

Aberdeen's growth as a fishing port began in the 1870's and was based on herring. At this time herring was caught by drifters such as the Fifies and Zulus. By 1918, most of the vessels operating were steam drifters. Drifting became less profitable during the 1930's as the market for herring declined.

Trawling was introduced to Aberdeen in 1882 and the city quickly became Scotland's biggest trawler port.

In the late 19th century many fishermen from local villages bought steam vessels for great line fishing rather than signing on as trawler crews. For many years, the city was Britain's biggest great line port accounting as much as 80% of the countries' total catch.

As an industry, during our period 1925 to 1955, fishing was central to Aberdeen with trawling, great line and seine netting, being the salient fishing methods employed. From the landing of fish to the fishmongers there spread a large infra-structure of service industries; net making, box making, ice making and canning etc.

Trawlers, Aberdeen harbour

Ted Munro: There wis practically three types o' fishin'. There wis fit y' caed the *'Sunday boat'*, the *'scratchers'*. They left here on Monday mornin' they were back on Wednesday. They went away Wednesday forenoon, they were back on Saturday then they hid the weekend at home. Then y' get the boats that were runnin' t' the West coast roond aboot the Shetlands, Orkneys roond the North Sea who went awar for maybe eight t' ten days. Then there wis the boats that wis goin' t' Iceland or Faroe.

David: What about a Faroe run in the Winter.

Ted: Y' get t' Faroe in aboot three hundred an' sixty mile. It would take aboot two days t' get there. If you were fishin' in the winter time you were in a lotta darkness, you would shoot the trawl at say four o'clock in the efternoon. You'd maybe hae a cuppa tea before it started. Now y' pull the trawl at maybe seven o'clock at night. At this time that y' pulled the trawl you'd hae y' supper. Then you'd g'forard into the pond an' start guttin' the fish. By the time you finished guttin' the fish you were towin' fer three hours an' it would be maybe half past eleven when y' shot again. Three hoors frae then you would pull that trawl again but durin' the space you wis guttin' the fish. By the time you gutted the fish, washed it an' got et below, you'd maybe a hoor an' a half before y' pulled the trawl the next haul.

So, y' went t' yer bed fa an hoor an' a half. Y' might be called again at half past two, or maybe half past three in the mornin' t' do the same process, pull the trawl, empty the cod end, throw the trawl over the side again.

"Heaving the lead" and the new echo meter

Sam West: When I started trawlin' they had no echo meters an' no wireless. When y' went intil the wheel house there wis the wheel, the telegraph an' a compass. That's the reason that s' many ships went ashore before this things (echo meters) come oot like. I startit trawlin' in 1933 an if y' wis awa oot t' the east an' comin in y' had t' soond the water t' find out far y' really was. At the end o' y' trip y' trawler wis light an' t' sound the water, if there wis ony wind at a' you'd t' keep them up through the wind because t' sound thirty fathom in the wind y' wouldna get the right soundin' with a hand lead. Fen y' come near the shore y' slowed doon especially if it wis foggy weather an y' started hearin' the fog horns. If it wis the Aberdeen fog horn that y' picked up well y' jist steamed awar from that but the fog horns were affa deceivin' in the mist. If y' picked up the Buchan Ness fog horn, well y' kent y' wis nae far between Aberdeen an' Peterhead. I was on the first trawler oota Aberdeen wi a wireless on. We were workin' the West coast affa Stornawar an' we had a wireless operator on board but there was no one with a wireless, the only fellas y' could speak til' were Fleetwood ships an' Hull trawlers. An' then they brought oot the echo meter which was affa poor for a kick off. If y' wis goin' astern y' see the echo meter wouldna work because the air bubbles was commin' underneath the ship so the echo meter wouldna work. It took the skippers a good while to understand that the echo meters wouldna work if y' wis goin' astern. The echo meters cam in aboot 1937. The wireless, telephone cam in aboot 1935. The hull boats an' the Grimmies carried a wireless operator but they had big crews, fifteen or sixteen of a crew. Well the Aberdeen boats didna have the telephone. It was aboot three month efter at before the first Aberdeen trawler got one.

On a trawler you'd ae y' gear t' mend. An affa lot o the time in the winter if y' wis steamin' y' couldna go on the deck 'cause y' deck wis awash most o' the time. When you got a bit heavy wi fish on a trawler an' there wis half a gale y' deck wis awash all the while especially when y' were steamin'.

When I was goin' trawlin' it wis different t' what it is now. You'd a fleet a boats that worked the North Sea on the inshore grounds, you'd a fleet a boats that worked the Shetland grounds, an' another fleet o' boats that worked Fairer (Fair Isle) an' there were a few boats that worked Iceland. Now if you worked at Iceland, most o' the boat went Iceland in the month o' March an' the month o' April. If y' went t' Iceland it took y' sixty hoors t' get there dependin' on the weather. Now we had three watches. We used t' hae two deckies, a watch if y' wisna near land but if y' wis near land it had t'be either the mate at wis in charge or the second fisherman same as the leadin' seaman in the navy. The second fisherman was above a deckie he wis between the mate an' the deckie. He'd an insurance ticket he'd nae a Board o' Trade ticket. The Board o' Trade rules was, two men had t' be on watch all the time. Y'canna do that now 'cause they're only carryin' four or five o' a crew. When I was workin' they were carryin' ten t' twelve.

Sam West's boat the River Esk

Simon Spalding: So you've got ten men, there's a skipper —

Sam: Skipper, mate, second fisherman, two deckies, maybe three deckies, engineer, chief engineer, second engineer, some of them had two firemen some o' them had one fireman. Y'd nine t' ten o' a crew.

Simon: Ah, you were coal fired ah, right ok.

Sam: Now them with the two firemen wis whut you called the 'after ender' jobs. Now y' boiler, y' see, if y' wis on a 'fore ender', what they call a fore ender job, the furnaces were at the fore end next t' the bunkers so y' didna need s'much trummen (carrying of coal). If y' wis in an after end, the boiler wis next t' th' engine so that fen y' fire started goin' down you'd t' carry coal fer the bunker t' the end o' the wing and then from the end o' the wing along t' (the furnace?) —

Simon: Seems an awful lot o' shovelling coal t' me.

Sam: Well, that's the reason they carried two firemen an' ca'd them after ender jobs. Y' the steamers forra start the bilers were a' aft but they foond oot efter a while it wis a lot handier with the doors (of the boilers?) forard. An' a lot o' trawlers, especially outa Grimsby hed the wheelhoose on top o' the galley. They used to call them 'bicycle boats' 'cause the wheel hoose wis on top o' the galley. But then they did awa wi that an' pit the wheel hoose in the centre the same as a' the rest o' the trawlers.

Simon: Y' didn't mention a cook —

Sam: Oh, that's another, - we had a cook, every trawler carried a cook. An' a' that he did wis cook.
He'da come into the 'pond' if we wis goin' heavy fishin' an' if he'd a bitty o' time off he'da come in an' gutted but he wis mostly in the galley all the time.
That's the trawler I wis on (indicating a photograph) the River Esk. She wis a hundred an' fifteen feet

in the keel an' she had beam twenty three or twenty four feet. She's entirely different t' the ships that's goin aboot noo. When y' shot y' net, y' see, y' towed. Skipper wida been in the wheel hoose an' then a deckie wid a gone on watch. Ye hid to pit in an hour in the bridge you'd be goin' fast before the hour wis up, you'd t' go up again to the next time that ye were shot. And ye did an hour for a watch, it wis a'right if ye wisne among too many boats but if y' wis among a lotta boats you'd t' keep y' eyes open because y' were goin' out an' in. An' they were towin' gear and y'had t'mak sure y' didna catch the other fellas gear.

Fen y' wis workin' y' gear y' stopped, — y' see at 'at time it wis all side trawlers now it's all stern trawlers. At that time y'stopped an' pit y' doors out, y' trawl doors then y' pit y' net ower the side. A lotta times when it wis bad weather you'd a stopped wi the doors on the lee side, tak aff the lashin' aff the trawl then the skipper wida come aheed onta the weather side wi the gear. Threw the net ower the side then y' slacked away the 'sweeps' (wires between the doors and the net) opened the doors, took oot the chains, y' slacked the doors inta the water. Then y' went ahead, skipper wis in the wheel hoose an the foredoor had t' shoot aff the side. The afterdoor had t' shoot in. One door went oot an' the other door went in. An' when they were like at y' started t' slacken awar the warps. You'd two fellas at the warps y'see. Now they could heave up with oot onybody t' winch at a 'cause they can do it wi press buttons fa the bridge. They were steam winches we used t' heave up but fen y'shoot y'gear y' had arthing oota gear an y' wis jist slackin' awar yer warps. The warps wis marked every twenty five fathoms. When they com oot, y' second fisherman, he was at the winch like, he kept this eyes on the marks so that they were equal.

Top: Trawler deck, showing the winches
Bottom: Trawlers fill Aberdeen Harbour

Now when y' had all y' warp oot, say y' had two hundred fathom, y' hid t' heave y' warps in - *(2 warps together; a hook with a wire attached was led to the winch which pulled them into a block at the stern of the ship)* - you'd a messenger t' go forrard owra the tap o' the after warp an' it hooked inta the fore warp. Y' pulled es in the fella fed it onta the winch. Now it's different a't'gether they dinna need a messenger or nothin' like that because they work the warps ower the stern. It's a lot easier.

The steam trawlers that I was goin' on wis a lot handier than the diesel trawlers because if you wis heavin' up wi a swell the steam woulda hove quick when she wis listin' towards the gear, - when she wis listin' awar from the gear she slowed doon but a diesel doesna dae that an' that's the reason that a lotta boats wis gettin' lost. Goin' fast an' you're heavin' up, wi a diesel they dinna slack they pull the boat doon.

Wi a diesel there is no come an' go as you've got wi steam it's got constant torque.

Simon: Tell me something about the music on board.

Sam: Fen the wireless come in it did awar wi a' that mostly. But the boat I was on; we used t' go inta Lerwick wi bad weather an' oor cook he wis a great fella fer the fiddle an' the melodeon. An' he ae used t' play at a dance in Lerwick. So this time we wis goin' in, he said t' me, - he ae kept his fiddle in the after bed because that wis ae empty y' know - he said, "I' better look at ma fiddle t' see fit like it is." He took het oot an' the back o' the fiddle wis aff! He got het sortit agen, glued on agen. When I startit t' sea most o' the ships hed a instrument a some kind. A melodeon an' fit d' y' ca' that eight sided things?

Simon: Concertina.

Sam: Aye, a concertina. What started comin' on the go wis the guitars, they startit comin on the go but they werna very popular at 'at time in the nineteen thirties. But the melodeon an' the fiddle were the most popular an' there wis often a mooth organ on board an' sometimes someone had a Jews harp.

Simon: Would you play them on board in fair weather?

Jesse Watts' fathers crew

Sam: Sometimes, there wis one skipper as I was wi, he used t' play the fiddle when we wis mendin' the deck but he wis one o' these exceptionally good fellas. This fella I wis tellin' y' aboot he wis up on deck, a fine day it was, wi an accordion like. We wis mendin' the deck an' a Hull trawler was goin' past an we took a photograph o' this Hull trawler an' he took a photograph o' us.

Simon: Looking at the photograph here, where was the accommodation etc.?

Sam: Oor accommodation wis doon here, half the crew wis doon here an' there wis four or five slept forard here in the fo'c's'le. This is the toilet here, see it stickin' up here but naebody used the toilet it wis ae bunged up. There wis nae toilet doon stairs either. What y' did fen y' wis on a steam trawler, y' went into the stoke hole an' took a shovel o' coal y' did y' job in the coal an' shovelled it on the fire. It wasna safe to go onto the rail in bad weather, - an awfa lot o' men lost their lives like at.

Simon: A Danish skipper said t' me that half the men that drowned at sea, if you could find their bodies they would have alcohol in their blood and their flies undone. (Laughter)

Sam: When we wis fishin' an' we wis goin' heavy fishin' 'specially the years jist after the war. You'd be workin' the deck for twenty four, twenty eight hoors. Never in your bed at a'. Now if y' were along wi a decent skipper he wid a said, "Take her aboard an' we'll lie fer half a dozen hoors." Now fen he wis lyin' fer half a dozen hoors the engineers woulda kept their eyes because he wisna steamin aboot y'see, they'd a kept their eyes on her. A' body wis turned in, sleepin'. But that wis only when y' wis with a good skipper. If y' hadna got a good skipper, - there wis a boat outa Aberdeen here, there wis seventy two hoors on the deck. There wis four men fell awar on the deck an' they were teen aff by the Communists an' they pit oot a couple o' leaflets aboot it.

A lota people frae Fraserburgh and Gardenstown from the fishin' community went t' Shetland because they could fish around the fiords or lochs, whatever they call it with oot goin' into the middle o' the sea. That wis fen the sail boats were on the go so it wisna so dangerous as it was fishin' at hame. In fact, there wis a lota poverty at 'at time. Even though you'd got fish it didna mean t' say you'd got money. A lotta times y' landed fish an' the market wis hopeless. A long time here in Aberdeen after the sail was past there wis es much bloody fash left in the market nae selt. At used t' be a common thing. Then they startit t' pit dye on them because some o' them were takin' the fish an' sellin' em underhand. There used t' be five hundred trawlers in Aberdeen but its supply boats that y' see now.

Alec Dey: The first boat I went on I wis aboot seventeen an' it wis called the Banks O' Dee. The skipper had the name o' bein' a notorious poacher roond the West coast, he'd sneak in an' poach, there wis nae raiders or naethin'. There were nine o' a crew on what we called an after ender jobs. That was the biler which was back t' front. They were little boats aboot ninety five feet, - the boilers, two furnaces an' the bunkers wis in the wings. One each side o' the boiler an' then there wis a little space f' some mair coal, at the back o' the biler up t' the wings far the coal could run doon an' through a door in t' the stoke hole an' let the engineer fire. The only light was from what we caed a 'bubbly'. Y' filled this little thing, a little lamp wi coalsea (sic) oil. It wis like paraffin bit thicker. It wisna supposed t' smoke s' much but the blummin' thing did smoke. It wis jist the bare flame, y' hang it up an that wis yer only light. If it wis an awfa bonny day y' might have aff the bunker lid. That wis the lids on the deck, y' screwed aff the lid an' got a bit o' fresh air in an' light.

Ted Munro: It wis like tryin' t' throw coal up Market Street! From the bottom t' the top! I only did one trip in an after ender job at wis a'.

David: What was so difficult about it Ted?

Ted: Wi a conventional trawler, the furnaces, y' had t' go through between the wing bunkers an' the boiler t' get t' the furnaces but in an after ender job the furnaces were nearest the engine. It wis alright if y' were on the coal pile by the wing it wis only one throw but once the wings got down t' the floor level y' t' go intae the main bunker an' you'd t' throw it from the main bunker t' the wing an' from the wing t' where the main bunker could get it!

David: How many people would have been doin' that ?

Ted: One man. One fireman got a shillin' a day extra but if y' got two firemen that shillin' came off.

David: So how many hours did you throw coal for?

Ted: Depends how much the ship was burnin'.
A watch, y' didna get four hoors as a recognised watch, five hoors 'cause by the time y' got the trawl shot you were goin' t' tow the trawl f' three hoors. You'd t' move all the coal the engineers wanted in that three hoors. If y' didna you'd t' go back after you'd a shot the trawl the next haul.

Alec: I started trawlin' in 1933. The best job of a' wis a Faroe boat especially in the summer time 'cause y' only did two hauls at night an' lay a' day. Fen the day light cam in a' the fish come off the bottom y' wouldna get nae fish durin' the day. So you'd only get two hauls maybe three at night.
After the war when the diesel boats cam in they fished night an' day 'cause the fuel was very cheap. I think it wis only sixteen poond a ton. It wis that cheap they kept goin'. That's why the grounds was kinda ruined.

George Lieper: I started fishin' when I was seventeen. It wasn't trawling that I did it was great line fishing. Great line fishing was a specialised job. We fished away at Faeroes and Iceland. Iceland was my happy hunting ground. You shoot your lines, maybe ten miles o' lines an' they lay along the bottom of the sea. They were made of Italian hemp, very strong stuff and you shot them in the morning. Any time between three o'clock an' six o'clock in the morning. Then y' started t' haul those lines back after about three hours and you were the whole day takin' them back. They were baited as they went over the side and as a bait for the first few days we possibly used herring but then efter that we used a special fish called a tusk an' we used t' cut it up into small portions an' use that as bait.

('Tusks and dollops' - A 'tusk' was a small fish akin to a small ling; these were cut into pieces 750mm to 850mm long and 250mm wide and called 'dollops'.)
We had twelve o' a crew, previously it had been eleven, 'cause durin' the war they caught fish in quantity. Now the head of a fish takes up a lotta room an' it's no use so you threw it away. Therefore they took an extra man who was employed t' tek off all the heads off the fish so they wouldna tek up the amount o' room in the fish hold. If you get a big cod the head's over a foot long. That would be cut off and thrown over the side leaving room for more edible parts o' the fish. So that wis the reason that we had an extra man.

David: What were the conditions like on board?

Ted: Well, t' my idea, the old Smokey Joes as they call them, y' lived in the fo'c'sle. I don't know about the cabin, but in the fo'c'sle y' lived like animals. Definitely, I quite believe that a lot o' animals were kept in better conditions. The owners didna bother aboot the sorta conditions you were livin' in. All they were worried aboot was gettin' the ship t' the sea t' catch fish. Some o' the conditions in that trawlers hid t' be seen t' be believed. You wouldn't believe it. This man wis talkin' aboot the Doonie Braes'. I wis fireman in the Doonie Braes' wi a Torry bloke, Davie Butters. Young Davie Butters was an awfa man fen he wis a fire man. An' I dinna ken how it happened bit the shackle that wis in the anchor cable hid been pit on upside doon. The pin that went through the shackle that joins the links together was uppermost. So the first time that we dropped the anchor the shackle came up an' ripped up the floor. When you went doon the companion way, there wis no floor. You'd to hang on t' the hand rail t' get y' feet on t' the side. It wis ripped up by the anchor it was repaired temporarily but as long as I wis on the Doonie Braes' there wis nae a proper floor.

Top: Press coverage of trawlermens grievances
Bottom: Building up steam

David: Did you get the rivets weeping water?

Ted: Oh aye, but it didna touch you in yer bunk. That went doon inta the forepeak but there was no means t' pump that water outa the forepeak an' maybe that water lay there nine month. Above it they kept tar, tallow, paraffin, everythin' that wis used wis kept in there an' this is where you slept.

When y' went on board, y' wore maybe a blue suit an' a jersey an' y' shoes. Then y' folded it up an' put it under y' pilla, there wis nae wardrobes, then y' pit on y' sea gear. We never changed oor underwear an' y' slept in your trousers. You'd be sittin' guttin' fish, an' when y' went t' bed all y' did wis teck off y' seaboots, off yer jersey an' inta bed. When I went away apprentice, the skipper I went away with, he'd a Mad McPherson. He said, "If you're goin' t' be a good trawl fisherman it's quite easy y' could be a good farmer. So I'd advise y' to be a farmer not a fisherman." Now he saw that I always washed ma hands after every drag of fish. I went inta the engine room an' got a bit o' soft soap. When I come ashore my hands were as clean as they are now.

Alec: Well I wis thinkin' some anecdotal things about the fo'c'sle. I remember once we went doon t' the hood, I was there livin', we were goin' awar t' sea an' they had painted out the fo'c'sle the day before and it wasn't dry so we had t' wash aff the paint wi paraffin afore we could get awar t' sea.

David: What about the crew and drinking?

Alec: It was all dependin' on the skipper. Some o' the skippers dished oot an' if you drunk at 'at wis you. Then they got echteen cases o' somethin', it was a fantastic amount o'drink. At wis efter the war, before the war, - efter y' went through the Pentland Firth y' never cracked the bond seal (duty free) till you were through the Pentland Firth if y' wis gaen t' Faerer or Iceland.

David: So what was it like to be on a posh boat then?

George: When a crew of a line boat joined at the new year time they knew, they were on that vessel for a whole year an' we looked on it as a home not jist as a place of work. We looked on it as a home an' we kept it clean, tidy an we didn't have the same experience as these two had. Ted will vouch for that 'cause he was a few years on the lines.

Ted: Yes.

George: And actually, four or five o' us slept in te fo'c'sle, that's in the prow o' the ship. That was a triangular area about ten feet in width in a triangle but it was always kept clean.

David: Who did the cleaning?

George: The fireman did all the cleaning. He very, very seldom worked in the forenoon so he did all the cleaning in the forenoon every day.

Ted: I kent an awfa difference comin' aff a trawler an' on to a line boat. I wis fed up o' trawlin', I couldna say about Hull, Grimsby, Fleetwood, I had a spell in Shields trawlin'. In the majority o' fishin' ports the trawlerman was despised. They were little more than animals bit an awfa lota people condemned 'em without considering the conditions they lived in. It wis the conditions they were livin' in that caused it. I think it wis J. B. Priestley that said, that "Trawl fisherman were the last uncivilised people in the civilised race."

T' gie y' an instance, we hid a cook in the Fernbank (a line boat) 'at bought a flat. Now when y' bought a flat y' hid t' buy the furniture so, (since he didn't need it) we took the furniture doon t' the Fernbank, we took it a drift an' practically rebuilt it in the fo'c'sle. It wis like a wardrobe where y' hung up y' clothes there. You'd never think about that trawlin', you'd never think a washin' the floor trawlin' never mind anythin' else. It wis a difference between black an' white.

David: What made you want to move from trawling and go on to great line fishing?

Ted: Yes 'cause my father wis chief in the engine room, trawlin'. I heard him talkin' aboot the better conditions in the lines than there wis in trawlin, so I thought I'd hae a go at the lines. I startit great line fishing with George in 1935, the year I got married. There wis an awfa lot mair open space on the deck, things were cleaner, even the men on board it were different frae the men trawlin'. It wis a common thing in the lines seein' a man haein a wash. Y' never saw a man haein a wash trawlin'. I seen y' away f' a fortnight, they wid never hae a wash or a shave (sniggers). Bit the line men were different. A different breed o' men all agither.

David: What comments have you to say about that then Alec.

Alec: Well the whole work style was different. Trawlin' wis hard push all the time. The lines was a more civilised life all together because the lines aboard the ship belonged t' the fishermen an' wid dee naethin' daft t' throw awar their ain livelihoods they had t' buy the lines, an' pay f' arthing themselves.

A young Ted Munro at work on the line boat 'Fernbank'

An' then they were mair casyul in their wye they didna bash on. Every one or two skippers was famous fer, - I wis at Doonie Braes an' the skipper I wis wi was a boy caed Bobby Bruce an' he wis whut we caed a good livin' boy. He wis a member o' the Free Kirk an' we got a heap o' coal frae Peterheed an' Bodam an' they a' wanted t' get fishin' Sunday. So we used t' lie Sunday. Bit the cook hid t' work an' the engineer hid t' work.

The trawler men got a bad name, in the 1950's y' saw in the papers trawler men gettin' fined fa refusin' t' sail an' nae turnin' up. Before the war y' signed on but if y' didna want t' ging a didna even think y' bothered signing aff. They wisna half as strict 'cause there wis always plenty o' men. Then we had a group o' people come on after the war, youngsters, we caed 'em 'commandoes'. They did some hell of a things, these commandoes. When we come back efter the war we was astonished. In fact the skipper asked him fen he wis gaen awar, he'd asked some o' the crew. These young boys were a' the crews they could get. An' if they decided, - we once decided, we wis goin t' sail frae Point Law an' there wis the fireman on shore wavin' us aff! The discipline efter the war had kinda broken doon.

George: A typical day for me was, we started fishing at four o' clock in the morning, we were finished by half past six. We had breakfast an' then we turned in to our beds for a couple o' hours and then at about eight o'clock we started hauling our lines back. At eight o'clock (at night) we were still hauling those lines in. That's how much fish we were getting with ten miles of lines. Now next day again, or other days we could be hauled and finished at ten o'clock at night.

David: When did you eat?

Ted: Echt in the mornin' breakfast, one a clock fer y' dinna'. Six a clock, y' tea, then eleven a clock wis a late supper. Now the engineers, they regulated their watches to coincide with their meal hours but as far as y' crew were concerned, y' fishin' crew, meal hoors med no difference.

If you wis finished guttin fish maybe one a clock, quarter to one. Y' shot the trawl first then you'd hae yer dinna, well it wis two sittin's, the first table an' the second table because a' body couldna g' doon at once. Now that wis an hoor of your time gone. You were goin' t' tow fer three hoors, then you would start guttin' an' by the time y' finished guttin' you'd t' pull the trawl again.

David: So how long could you go with out sleep?

Ted: Till y' fell asleep at the table. That wis a common thing to see a man fall asleep at the table. When I was apprentice the skipper wis thinkin' o' tyin' me t' the hand rail because I had t' fill all the needles f' mendin' nets an' it wisna the first time that I fell asleep standin' on the deck fillin' needles.

George: Thirty six hours was about the limit. Y' could go two days but you'd be feelin' very tired. Our meal times were different. We had set meals, eight, one and six the same as them. Fishing time made no difference we had our meals at that time and the time we had for a meal was half an hour.

Alec Dey: Before the war we had t' pay for oor food. Once we had a cook an' he wis very cheap he wis once seven an' six for a week but we got fish twice a day. F' late supper he'd mak a hash wi corned beef an' spuds. Then there used t' be arguments because the skipper used t' have his ane grocer, some o' the Torry grocers, that they used t' say that there wis so much goin' up t' (his) hoose. An' they did that wi the butcher an a'. I'm sayin' this fer the sake o' fit actually happened. We used t' say the Lord sends the grub an' the Devil sends the cook!

Albert Hepburn: Well my first job was when I went to sea, my father asked me what I wanted to do when I was fourteen an' I sez well, I'd like t' either go to a farm or go t' sea. Well he took a man over to see me when I was fourteen like, a farmer, an' he comes into the hoose. I never seen a scratch o' a man in all ma life. I thought that I was going t' ging to a ferm an' get fed up y' know wi a big red faced man comin' in to the hoose, a real ferma y'know. But this man comes in, he wis as thin as a poker an' I sez if you're a ferma I'll get little meat affa you. The man has a news t' me an' ma father an'

the man gis awar an' ma father sez 'whits the matter now, fit ye gaen t'de ?' an' I sez be the look o' that man he's in need o' a feed so I'm nae goin' t' ging wi him. So I sez I'll ging t'sea, so he went doon t' auld Torry an' got a pair o' auld sea boots. That's whit I went awar t' sea with. Fen I gid aboard the boat a' the other chaps were wearin' leather boots, they musta thought I come oota a midden or something.

Joyce: How old were then ?

Albert: Fifteen, jist fifteen past.

Lizzie: Did you leave school fen you were fourteen ?

Albert: Fourteen.

Lizzie: Fit wis your first job at fourteen then ?

Top: Stocking up with bread
Bottom: Aberdeen Fish Market

Albert: Well I worked in Smith's nurseries far the infirmary is now, in 1924. There was a lot o' us weedin' an' plantin' an things like at. I think there wis four o' us picked oot. They grew big raspberries at that time, eatin' raspberries like, an it wis a twenty four hoor service an' fit we had t' do wis to be on duty for six hoors or something like at and ye got a handfu o' little steens an' you'd t' throw this at the birds which come doon t' pick the strawberries. And frae there we went up t' Hazelhead.

The conditions when I went to sea were very poor. We slept in the fo'c'sul and aft o' the fo'c'sul where you slept wis the place where you kept all the paraffin for the lights, an' the tarry nets an' the smell used t' be terrible. Y'ken when y'went awar in the auld trawlers, they were open decks y'see and if she took a big lump o' water, well there wis water splashin' doon the stairs. So you wis bad t' sleep wi that commin' under the door.

Joyce: I've heard my father sayin' when he'd been awar on a new boat, when he cam hame, me mither wis sayin' 'Fit like it wis?', an' he'd say 'I wis ae sleepin' wi me sea boots on', because the water would be comin' in fen autumn oota abeyance there'd be several inches o' water.

Lizzie: There was one time my grandfather wis washed oot be a wave an' washed back by the next.

Joyce: Well my father landed up in the hospital in Lerwick wi jandice because there'd been rats in the water. Ma husband, he got that rat fever an' a'. That aul doctor Leiper he come in to see ma husband but he couldna decide fit wis a dee with him an' Bob was gettin yellower an' yellower and it was a young doctor that cam in sine an' he said, 'Far do you work?', he (Bob) sez, 'The fish'. 'Ah, that's it' (Said the doctor.) That rat fever wis very bad in the fish hooses where maybe they'd lay their piece doon or something far a rat had been.

Albert: Well I worked in the fish and there wis thousands o' them. I workit next to Mellis' an' they used to come frae there into the fish hoose an' I've seen me stanin' there in the middle o' the flear, at one o' clock efter a' the machinery was aff they used t' run roond yer feet an' jumpin' an' they were that size!

Women braiding fishing nets at home in 1946

Lizzie: The sanitary used t' come roond an' put doon rat poison an' fen the rats took the poison they went t' water. There wis ae tubs o' water in the fish hoose. Well the first thing you did fen y' gid in in the morning, you pit on yer oil skins an' y' washed it, y' wet it, that was t'save the fish scales sticking till it. So I went in an I went to wash it doon wi a bit o' sackin' you'd dip it in the water an' sluice it ower, an I went like this, sluice, sluice, an' then I looked an' I had a rat in my hand nae a bit o' rag! It wis dead o'cause, it had been poisoned and I jist flung it. Well, I washed ma hands in cold water, I should have used disinfectant. That wis me, I almost died.

Joyce: .... used t' bring a mannie from the country wi a ferret an he used to let het loose in the fish hoose an' by golly it jist got them by the scruff o' the neck and shook them to death.

Lizzie Findlayson: *(from a letter)* When I was a young girl I would fill the large wooden needles with twine for my aunt Maggie. I would receive three old pennies for each ball I finished. My aunt's husband was a fisherman so that when he was at sea she could make much needed extra money by making trawl nets.* The work could be done at home, with the twine being delivered one week, while the finished nets collected the following week and more material left. In summer the women would hammer large hooks into the outside walls and work in the air. The hooks supported the rod which held the net, which was lifted and re-threaded on the rod when it became too long to braid in comfort.

Occasionally my aunt would take time to teach me the art of weaving. With a spool in one hand and a twine filled needle in the other, I soon picked up the process. Once I was good enough my aunt let me work on her net, decreasing or increasing as required.

However, it wasn't till I married in 1934 that I started doing nets at home. Married women didn't go out to work at that time, and I needed the extra money to purchase various items for the home. I started on mending squares for McKenzie, ship chandlers of Sinclair Road. Those were used by fisherman to patch any tears in the nets when at sea. They measured 100 mesh in each direction, wages were 30 shillings per square. In no time I could do any kind of net, wings, bellies or cod ends, the last one being done in double twine throughout. The various pieces were joined together by men, on the ship chandlers premises.

*See also page 58 **'Far wis ye fin the sireen blew'**.

NET-MAKING does not attract young girls as it used to do, and a labour crisis is only being averted by willing "old hands"—many of them married and with grown-up families—who keep up production by working in their own homes. Above- Mrs M. Bracewell, Grampian Circle, fills her needle with twine before starting another section. Below- George Whyman, who first went to sea sixty years ago, keeps up his connection with the fleet by assembling the nets at the premises of W. McKenzie & Sons, Ltd., ship chandlers, Sinclair Road, Aberdeen. George was a trawl skipper for forty-eight years, and there is nothing the young 'uns can teach him about this job.

When war started in 1939 many fishermen joined the navy. This meant that fewer trawl nets were needed, so we turned to camouflage nets instead. From a factory in Stonehaven we were sent rough flax, like twine, with which to do the camouflage nets for the forces. At £1 per net I could make £6 or £7 per week, which was good pay at that time. One hundred mesh decreasing to one, turn and do the same at the other side, making a huge diamond, large enough to cover a gun. They had leaves and branches put through the mesh by the forces members, so it was camouflaged and not noticed from the air.

We had to go to Grimsby stores on Saturday forenoons for our pay, woe betide anyone who caught two loops together. There it was written in ink on the envelope (caught in mesh). If this happened a few times, one was threatened with dismissal. He was a very particular gentleman Mr Johnstone.

Jesse Watt: We did twenty one feet cod ends and twenty four feet cod ends in double sisal sometimes 125 and 150 in double sisal with a two and a half inch spool. And they were twenty four feet. We startit at a hundred came inta fifty an' then y' worked from that till they were twenty four feet or twenty one feet fit ever size y' wis doin'.

Trevor Davies: Where did you do your work?

Jesse: Well doon at the harbour there wis a lot in the stores, there wis Enterprise, there wis the Grimsby stores, the Bon Accord Mutual, Walkers Stores, there were quite a number o' net stores.

I started at the Bon Accord Mutual when I wis fifteen. It wis piece work, so much for a cod end, so much for top wings an' lower wings. There wis different pieces of the net that y' did and the riggers made up the trawl with the bits that the girls did.

The men were the riggers we didna make up the nets, the riggers made up the nets, pit on the bobbins an' what have y'.

Trevor: How did you make them, a needle, or what?

Top: Assembling nets at W. McKenzie & Sons, Sinclair Road, Aberdeen
Bottom: Jesse Watt's father

Jesse: They were wooden needles that we used about nine inches long and y' filled y' needles and y' had a spool on your hand and y' jist worked like that.

Ina Mair: It wis nae jist cod ends it wis wings an a'.

Jesse: Yes it was top wings an' lower wings and what they called bellies and the battens.

Ina: A belly wis thirteen shillin's.

Trevor: How long did it take you to make?

Florence Cumming: It wid a teen y' aboot three days onyway. Three or four days.

Trevor: What time are you talking about?

Florence: Before the war, about 1938. We used t' cheat. Your work had t' be done before a certain time before you could get your wage. We used t' sneak oot some o' the twine and you'd maybe do the battens that went on to the cod end. That gives y' five shillin's more. So that instead o' goin' out wi a pound y' went oot wi twenty five shillin's, then y' sneaked it back in jist before the time. Nearly everybody did it, we did at the Enterprise.

Ina: Y' had t' do things like that in that days, for an extra shillin'.

Florence: And y' jist hoped that y' wouldna get caught when y' came back wi it tied aboot yer waist. (laughter)

Trevor: Did anyone get caught?

Florence: No, I think they turned a blind eye to it, they knew that you were bringing in the stuff that you were doing at home. It wis only when y' did yer cod ends that we did that.

Jesse: But mind you it was a happy job. Because you used t' sing most o' the day when you was workin'. Everybody sang, it was the same in the fish hooses.

Trevor: What were the songs you sang?

Jesse: Sometimes we sang hymns and sometimes you had the modren songs, we jist sang.

Florence: Sometimes, when someone was reading a good book, an' they spoke about this book, well whoever had t' sit in to fill their needles they wid continue with the story an' we used t' sit and have your book like that while they were workin' their nets an' the person who was fillin' their needles read the story. If ony body was throwin' their needles in the basket, y'ken who they clicked, well they startit t' pitin a sack into the basket so they wouldna click so we could hear the story.

Jesse: Sometimes the Peoples Friend used t' be awfa popular fa readin', it was a very happy job.

Trevor: What was the place like where you worked?

Ina: It wis jist a loft, a long narrow loft.

Florence: We'd a big room, a bay window, it looked right oot on the fish market.

Jesse: The nets were hung up on the wall then y' took up y' row there an' pit it up agen.

Trevor: Were the nets hung on nails?

Ina: No, there wis hooks -

Jesse: No, no, don't say nails!

Ina: An' an iron bar. You'd do a length then you'd shift it up agen.

In the fish sheds.

Lizzie Findlayson: I started in George Angus fish house at eighteen. The wages were 6 pence (2.5p) an hour, but after a few weeks I was upgraded to 8 pence (3.3) an hour. It was a Tuesday morning I started, having gone to Fiddes on Monday to ask for my lie days wages. This came to 12 shillings (60p), and I went to Grimsby's stores for the necessary oilskins. There wasn't enough money left for rubber boots, but I got the loan of a pair of leaky wellingtons from a neighbour which saw me through till Saturday. My first wage was just over £1 and I went straight to town from work on Saturday. I purchased rubber boots for 14 shillings (70p) as my pocket money was now 5 shillings (25p) weekly my mother got no wages from me that week, which didn't please her.

I was sick for a whole week, until I became accustomed to the various smells. I learned all the processes as time went on and soon became a smoker, starting with the peats then with smoked finnans as a turner. For this I got an extra 2/6 (12.5p) if I worked on Saturday afternoons. I worked in the smokey house, later, where the fish and haddock were actually cooked over a pit. This time the fire was wood chips, a huge bag for each kiln. Sawdust sprinkled on top made the smoke. The fish were tentered in pairs tied together by the tails, then slung across the open pit. Clean sacking was thrown across the top, through which water would be sprayed to keep the fish moist while cooking. I liked the work. If the market was poor, we would be sent home, but even with that I had more wages than before.

I learnt to do net braiding in my spare time which was to be handy later on in life. I left George Angus at 26 years of age to be married.

Woman: I workit in the fish sheds from when I was fourteen till I wis sixty nine. I only had time off t' have ma children. An' it was the happiest time o' ma life.

Trevor: Wasn't it cold and wet though?

Woman: Oh, yes. It wis cold but it was very friendly an' we sang all the time. T' start with I had eight shillin's which is forty pence that wis my pay for the week. I had that for the year then when I went on to skinin' (I startit finnin' at first, tekin the fins aff) I got it up t' ten shillin's.

Trevor: How did y' take the fins off?

Woman: Y' cut the bottom bit off then y' went up the two sides and pulled aff the fin then they got in the machines efter that. I did all sorts a different fish there wis block fillet or single fillet. The single fillet is the two sides the block fillet is the whole fillet but there's two t' the single fillet of one fish y' see.

With halibut, which is a big fish, y' didna cut ony fins off y' jist y' cut the side startin' at the top an' g' right down. Then y' turned it over an' do the back an' skin the back. Y' skin a fish by takin' the tail and y' pull the skin an' move your knife an' the skin jist comes aff. The fins have t' be off or y' knife would stick y' see.

Trevor: When did you start working in the fish?

Woman: I was born in 1916 and started work in the fish in 1930.

We had t' get up early, an' we had very little for we a bit o' toast or something.

Woman: Ma mither used t' send me fa burst sausages an' she used t' put em together an' make a batter for em an' that was oor Sunday dinner. We used t' call em 'busters', a penny o' busters we got em cheap y' see.

Jean?: I worked in the Esplanade, the fish esplanade ... Phillips, I was there till I was twenty one. He was a good boss but we didna get much pay but neither did onybody else. But he was good, very good. There were aboot fifty people at the place I worked in. You weren't allowed t' smoke, y' got sacked on the spot if y' were catched smokin'. The girls were aboot fourteen or fifteen but they was really happy times 'though it was cold.

Trevor: Has it changed that much over the years?

Woman: Oh, yes they've got central heatin' in most o' the places now.

Woman: An' y' get y' het water dip.

Wages and unions in the fish.

Joyce: "Bob used t' say that the fishin' trade, they wouldna jine unions 'cause the unions wouldna let them work the hoors they did - my man workit fa six a'clock in the mornin' till six a clock at night, heed one wiks holiday, he workit on a Saturday till dinna time, he workit on a Sunday till dinna time. When he was at Peterhead an' Lossimooth an' a' that ken, I mean they'd nae really ony set hoors, like from nine t' five, an he said that nae trade union would let them do that an if they wouldna let them de it the fishin' trade would jist flop 'cause you've got t' work when the fish is there. If the fish is nae there, then fair enough, but if the fish is there then you've got to work.

Women packing Herring in barrels

Albert: But then again here wis me, goin' t' sea workin' twenty four hours a day for nine an' six (62.5p) an' when you counted it out it came to coppers. It was really scandalous. The highest I worked in a day (working shift) was fifty six hours and nae gettin' aff for yer food, the skippers wouldnae let you aff the deck we was busy mendin' nets, splicin' wires and ropes an' things like that.

Lizzie: Ma' be there was nae a union in them days you payed in till a penny a day, that covered compensation —

Albert: That was for your medical, ha, that was a different thing a' together.

Lizzie: When I wis eighteen, they used t' come rooned the fish places steady an' they would ask ye, 'Are ye gonna join a union?' And of course the bosses wouldna let us because it was a' private owned, every fish place wis owned privately, now the co-operative they had a union that wis the only fish place - an' Alan and Dey some o' the workers were members o' a union. I worked for McBey at Poynernook Road and no way - if you joined a union it was as good as askin' yer box. (the sack) Nae use, because they said the union asked too much.

Joyce: When my husband first came hame from the army, efter the war before he went t' the fish, he was workin' for Tawse the builder, puttin' in the drains at what is now Garthdee housing scheme, a wee shower o' rain an' he'd be hame an' o' 'cause y' didna get paid for it y' see, this was it. And efter he said to hang wi this I'm nae haein this, an' he left an' got a job drivin in the fish. And he used t' say I'll never join a union again.

Lizzie: It was the same in the fish trade as well Joyce, if there was nae fish in the market you were put hame. You were paid by the hour. Well I started at sixpence an hour an' I was eighteen so my average wage was about thirty eight shillin's (£1.90) . That was about the average wage at that time. I left Fiddes, when I was eighteen to ging t' the fish for mair money because they wouldna let me on to the piece work - this wis eighteen shillin's (90p) for one weeks work, we are spikin' in aul' money a' cause. It wasna much really startin' wi ten shillin's (50p).

Joyce: Do you mind Andrew Leiper the newsagent in Victoria Road, well that's where I started work, the week efter my fourteenth birthday an' I workit from seven in the mornin' till nearly eight at night some nights. An' I got six shillin's (30p) a week an' at the end o' the year he said, 'I'm awfa pleased wi ye I'm going t' gie ye a rise.' What did I get ? Six pence (2.5p)!

Lizze: Mind you sixpence (2.5p) would buy you a packet o' tea an' a packet o' sugar at 'at time.

Albert: At that time my mither would gie us tuppence (less than 1p) and an old basket an' send us across the road to ask for tuppence worth o' mixed vegetables. You'd get carrots, turnips, leeks, everything.

Joyce: Efter that I workit in McKeggie's at the top o' Union Street, the book sellers there an' I got twelve and sixpence (62.5p) there. And that was good money, then I gid into the army an' got nine shillin's (45p) a week.

SHIPBUILDING IN ABERDEEN

Shipbuilding in Aberdeen has a long established history. Alexander Hall was the oldest ship yard in the City during our period (preceding Hall Russell's by a good few years) building various types of dredgers, tugs, hopper barges, coasters and fishing vessels.

Hall Russell as a firm commenced building ships in 1864. Notably for the service between the United Kingdom and Australia. this company built the clipper Thermopylae in 1891. Not only did they have a reputation for building high class combined cargo and passenger vessels but they also played a pioneering part in the development of the modern trawler being responsible for the first motor trawlers in this country.

John Lewis was founded in 1870 and by 1907 it was the largest supplier of engines to the herring fishing fleets of North East Scotland, Lowestoft, and Yarmouth. During the First World War they were making minesweepers and salvage craft. In the 1930's they made colliers, coasters trawlers and cargo ships. The manufacture of the Lewis-Doxford diesel was one of the firms most prominent post Second World War developments.

Bill Shinnie: I was about seventeen or eighteen and that would have been about 1940 round about there. Well I got this job with Hall and company, the oldest shipbuildin' company in Footdee. I was with the carpenters an' the carpenter's job was t' set up the keel and the main framework of the ship, the ribs, get it all fixed up, bolted together then the platers came along. The platers bored the holes for the plates, fitted em, bolted them on. Then the riveters come in behind them and there was what we called a 'holder on'. He had t' go on inside the ship, he held the rivet from the inside an' the riveter did the job from the outside. Finally, he tapped the rivets into position and t' find out if they were cracked they used t' go about with a little hammer an' tap the rivets. If it wis faulty they'd mark it, tak that one out again an' replace it until eventually the ship wis built up, put on the slidin' ramps an' into the docks.

David: Did you work outside then?

Bill: Yes, I worked outside all the time. The scaffoldin' wis jist like three stumps with slots in them, battens pit through, battens laid across where y' could work at whatever level you wanted t' go to from the after-end t' the forepeak. Y' used the same scaffoldin' an' jist altered it t' the different heights 'cause the riveters had t' have different heights for holdin' their rivet guns up.

Archie Lennox: On certain jobs it was recognised that you got 'dirty money'.

David: And what's 'dirty money'?

Archie: And under certain circumstances we got 'risk money'.

David: Give me an idea Archie where you got 'risk money'.

Archie: Well, on ship buildin' where you went oot on repair work you could be equally dirty on new work if it was rusty plates that were bein' manipulated. If you went oot on repair work you had to contend with the nature o' the age and the deterioration and the different corners you had t' get into on the ship. For instance Aberdeen and its trawlers. The fish room sump was about the most horrible thing that you could tolerate, ken?

David: Describe it, Archie.

Archie: That's where the slime o' fish room went to an' the water was pumped oot but the slime was still there. The best y' could do was t' get bags o' sawdust, paraffin and naphtha, throw it around an' set fire to the place y'know. I could tell a story ...

> *"It's a pity it's all gone, an industry of good men who worked hard, played hard, and with exceptional skills - the ships proved that."*

David: Tell us a story then.

Archie: When I wis a boy in the First World War the squad was directed doon t' the Fittie pontoon and there was the Acasta and the Oslo (sic) come direct fae the Jutland battle an' put on t' that pontoon dock t' keep them fae sinkin'. The ships were damaged fa gunfire and were in sinkin' condition so they were put aboard the pontoon dock. Well my recollection o' it is bein' told t' stand by because we had a tidyin' up job t' do and at that time o' day plates that had t' come off the rivets had t' be cut out manually, there was no oxyacetylene in these days and er the heater boys, rivet heaters an' catchers were surplus to requirements so we were told t' stand by for a cleanin' job. A cleanin' job that never materialised but puttin' it all together later there was almost a revolt amongst the Navy men that were left on board the ship because what they were seekin' us t' do was t' g'doon into the engine room an' tidy up human remains that were there. That's how I remember it as a boy of fifteen or fifteen and a half.

David: Did anybody go aboard?

Archie: It was a usual squad o' labourers that had been passed and they were going to tie up by the buoy, but the crew men stepped in — and then the crew were put up to the sailor's home and they come off the ship all a gither and how it was tied it up in the end I don't know.

Walter Watt: My dad who was called 'Wattie' also worked on the yards at that time. He was a rivet catcher like myself as a young boy. Later he went t' work in the iron foundry. I remember him telling me about being sent with some more boys to clean out the ship. He said it was terrible especially in the engine room where there were bits of the sailors blown through the gratings like pounds o' mince, and boots with feet in them. The kids were all sick wi just looking never mind wiping up. I believe they were offered something like five bob as a bonus, disgusting. I can imagine how those lads felt - I saw the carnage in Hall Russells bombing and I was only fifteen.

Archie's son Tammy was a plater the same as me. I was his shop steward for many years. He was a die-hard member of the Communist Party and a good trade unionist. I can remember him telling me about his daughter as a young lass being very keen on music, little knowing she would become the famous star Annie Lennox.

Jim McCartney: Now ship building, y' had an average o' sixty apprentices a year. I was convener at Hall Russell's. The laddies came from Lewis' as well as Hall Russell's and the Wood Group they come in on the first day on the Monday and as convener, on the Tuesday, I addressed 'em and made it quite plain that they join the unions. They went home and told their Mum's and Dad's that, if they didna join a union they wouldna get here on Wednesday. It was always accepted. What we used t'do was t' give them three weeks wages an' they joined a union. Five bob t'jine an' ten pence a week or something like that, I canna remember exactly, and this built up a community spirit. If y' lived in Torry y'worked in Lewis'. If y' lived this side o' the Victoria bridge, y' worked at Hall Russell's or y' worked at the Wood Group or you worked in the little places roond aboot which have gone. Now we've lost all the apprentices through this.

Walter Watt: I walked into Hall Russells on the 8th o' February 1939. I wanted t' be in show business but ma dad said, "Y' nae goin' intae that poofy jobs." I don't know where I might have gone, I don't know, I think I could have made somethin' oot o' it 'cause I did become a semi pro comedian in the clubs an' I had a band y' know. I think he wis right though, the war wis not very far away. So ma dad sez, "No you'll have t' get a job." So, away I went doon t' Hall Russells with no career in mind, in ma

Advertisements for John Lewis & Sons Ltd.

flannels an' ma blazer. There was only one ship in the stocks, so I got a job as a rivet catcher. That's about the lowest o' the lowest that y' get as a little boy. Y' pick up a rivet an put it in the hole.

Trevor: The rivets would be hot though ?

Walter: The lad heats em in the fire, right? Throws em t' you, you pick em up wi a pair o' tongs an' y' pit it into the rivet hole. The holder-up, he's got a hammer, he holds it in an' the lad ootside's got a rivitin' gun.

It was terrible conditions, with the noise an' that. You'd no idea o' darkness or daylight, we jist looked through the rivet holes an' they'd shout an' swear at y'. I wis a timid wee soul, I wis terrified. It wis all carbide lamps, there was no electric lights an' you were right doon in the bowels o' the ship. We were on piece work and unless we produced hundreds o' rivets a day y' didna get paid. You had t' go wi 'em. Thursd'y was pay night we used t' go on the beer an' y' didn't go aff the ship t' go to the toilet either. Y' could imagine the smell when a hot rivet fell in among it. One day a hot rivet fell doon the back o' ma neck an' I'm screamin' an' he said, "Fits a do wi yea?" He jist turns me upside doon, shook oot the rivet an' that wis that! There was very little first aid, there wis very little medical treatment in shipbuildin' at that time, that came later on. There was some bad accidents an' some died an' er och, gettin'

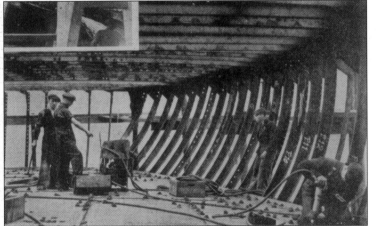

Top: Walter Watt at work - A. Hall & Co. Shipbuilders - 1949
Bottom: Riveters at work on a skeleton ship

burnt, I used t' go home sayin' I'm not goin' back. Dad sez, "It'll mak a man o' ya." I've seen young lads spirit broken, it wis rough and if y' didn't know their humour you'd had it. You'd have a bonnet, y' know I was so little I had ma Dads bonnet with a big pin. And a pair o' long Johns because it wis Winter an' it was cold, really cold. I've seen me cryin' wi the cold, no heatin' nothin', it wis jist not a beautiful place. Iron is a very cold very heavy stuff t' handle and you bend before that does.

Y' had to look after the holder-up's tools yer drifts and tongs an' y' had to carry the rivets. A half hundred weight o' rivets carried by a fourteen year auld, that wis some bloody weight. And y' had t' learn aboot the different sorts o' rivets and know what they were wantin'. When y' cam to three ply thick plate that wis what y' called a jointer. That wis a favourite sayin' in the shipyard, 'After five a jointer.' You hid t' shout t' the heater boy, "After five ordinary rivets a bigger rivet." We'd t' learn aboot cup heads, countersinks, panheads. So that's where y' start as a rivet catcher an' most of us start as a rivet catcher unless you were more refined and started as an apprentice.

Beatrice Sangster: I went down t' the Labour Exchange in Windmill Brae an' they offered me this job in Hall Russells an' I took it.
So when I went down they said, "You'll have t' have a boiler suit and tackety boots." So I had t' go t' the Co-opy in George Street an' get a boiler suit and boots.

David: So this was during the war. Was it unusual to see a woman in the shipyard?

Beatrice: It was mainly all women 'cause the men were away at the war. The first job I did was, I was pit on a pneumatic drill t' break up stones and then, we had t' make a road an' level it using a cement mixer wi chuckies an' sand. Layin' the stones. Then y' left it so long then poured it into a barra then some lady took the barra an' pit it on t' where they were makin' the road an' another lady took a shovel an' was levellin' it off.

David: This was a road that was in Hall Russells itself?

Beatrice: Yes it was literally out the side door through the yard. You were only allowed t' work there for about six months then I was pit on as a catcher wi the riveters. I had t' get rivets from the store, you'd t' climb a ladder on to the boat then I gave the heater boy the rivets and he heated em. Then there was a riveter above an' down the tanks wi me wis a holder on. I used t' catch the rivets put em up through the hole an' the ho'der on used t' ho'd em up an' the riveter used t' whack em down.

David: How did you catch the rivets?

Top: John Lewis shipbuilders, machine shop - 1920's
Bottom: Under construction at Hall Russell - shipyard A

Beatrice: With a big pair o' pliers, you'd t' catch em in this big pair o' pliers. Here's you lyin' flat on yer stomach puttin' the rivets up through the holes in the plates.

David: Was it just the catching that women did or did they do any of the hitting?

Beatrice: No jist catchin'. I worked with Jock Mackie, he wis the riveter. Doddy Bye (?) he was the hou'der on an' Gus Fraser he wis the heater boy an' I wis the catcher. We worked as a team the four o' us.

David: Where else did you work?

Beatrice: For war work, with Forbes' repairin' cars. We did trainin' in Castle Street. Did a few months trainin' there, it was all ladies and then we were sent oot t' different garages. That wis in 1944. The men didna accept ye, the men didn't like it, no. They made it really hard for yer. They were jist nasty t' ya. The younger ones, they jist didn't like y' workin' there. The older ones were nice, really nice but the younger ones didna like you bein' there. They jist ignored y' an' made nasty remarks an' things like that. We shouldn't be there, ladies shouldn't be workin' that work an' things like that but the older men they were really nice.

We worked on motorcars and vans and lorries and things like that there. It was a repair shop in Hutcheon Street. They were really nasty the young eens, y' couldna work there. I jist stayed a few months because they werena nice t' ya. There were only about two girls there. But I did like workin' in Hall Russells, I really did like workin' there.

David: It's a pity you had t' give that up then isn't it?

Beatrice: Well y' see the ladies were all paid off 'cause the men were comin' back from the war.

Walter Watt: I was on with one family, the Reynolds, a great family, father an' son. They would fight one another, spit at one another an' you were in between y'know an' you were scared. You were scared o' them. They used t' tease y' aboot women an' things like that. Y' didn't know what they were talkin' aboot half the time. The riveters had an old sayin' aboot pay night, an' they used t' speak aboot 'rum, bum, and tobacco night'. Well I knew about rum and tobacco but - "What's the bum?" "Shut up you've no need t' know aboot that!" was the reply. An' they teased ya, an' they did tease ya. Maybe you'd got a nice tidy jacket - "That's a nice tidy jacket oh yes, it's lovely buttons, do like that buttons?" "Yes I like that buttons." I replied. "Well here you are then!" pullin' the buttons aff ma jacket and giving them t' me! But give em their due, their humour was rough but as sure as hell somebody would bring doon a bonnet t' you. An' they were good t' yer an' ma pay wis ten shillings an' sixpence (This is weekly and equals about 52 pence) with four pence (less than 2p) off fer y' stamp. Eventually the gaffer cam t' me an' he sez "How wid yea like t' go wi the platers?" More money, fifteen bob a wik as a markin' boy. So, I went into the platin' shed an' I wis wi the same plater for a long time. My job was a ,- you'd a little flat thing called a 'batty o' peg'(?) y' dipped a bitta three-quarter tube or whatever size you were doin'. You had

Top: Alan Reid, Sid Davidson and Walter (holding chains)

battens wi holes in em an y' marked all this holes for the rivets. This is before the weldin' come in. To see a ship constructed, riveted, was very good. Piece meal, puttin' on the ribs first then yer stretcher shell, that's the skin shell then your deck, - we did it piece by piece. Halls was a very auld yard, very old fashioned. In 1939 there was very little doin' an' it wasna uncommon t' get paid off. You had to pay people off if there was no ship to build. Most kids would g' roond the yard collectin' old bolts an' washers, save money, and I'll always remember, I was standin at the bottom of the harbour, darkish kind, throwing stones at a bottle. A hand cam roon ma shoulder, this is the foreman Peter Lyon who became a manager. He wis a big man, massive, an' he said, "Now lad we can't have that, go and get your books." I startit cryin', "If y' give me ma books ma dad'll kill me!" Anyway, I got ma books an' ma stamps, they were jist lookin' for an excuse t' lay folk off. So I went home to tell the old man in the Castlegate y'know. So I went home, plucked up courage, an' I sez t' dad "I got paid off tonight." "You're a bloody liar, y' didna get paid off y' got bunged. They don't pay off kids." I said, "I did, I did." "If I thought y' got the bung laddie I'll thump ya from the back o' the wa'" An' he was quick at that believe you me. They depended on gettin' my pennies as well, ma dad was only a caretaker so he sez, "Get another job." So the next day I went doon t' Halls door along York Street a bit. I wis in the door there an' the foreman riveter cam up. Mr. Hogg was his name. "Well laddie fit can I do for y?, have y' worked in the yard before?" I sez, "Aye I were next door." "What was ya." "A rivet catcher," I sez. Then a riveter cam up, Reynolds, "I'll hae that wee boy, I've had him before he's alright." So I wis set on wi the platers.

The war came on and I had the great grandeur of becoming a Battle o' Britain pilot. I was in the air cadets y' see and I planned t' be an air gunner actually but I ended up being a ground gunner. Anyway time went on wi the platers, y' couldna leave 'cause the war was on an' I wis workin' three nights and

Saturday an' Sunday. I wis only fifteen be that time an' one day the gaffer sez t' me, "What are you workin'?" I sez, "Three nights Saturday an' Sunday." He sez, "You're too young t' work at." An', I sez, "Well, I jist follow ma tradesman, the plater an' he jist tells me t' come oot." He sez, "Well jist tak aff the Seterdy mornin'!" It was an eight hour day but when y' worked in the evenin' y' got a break for half an hour then y' worked on till aboot nine o'clock, ten o'clock. At one time y' worked on Saturday mornin's that was normal procedure. Saturday afternoon was overtime, Sunday wis overtime but because o' the war it was compulsory. When I was about sixteen the foreman plater cam t' me an' said, "Would y' like t' serve your time?" (As an apprentice.) To be an apprentice y' had t' sacrifice the pay but the war helped wi the overtime. I went home an told ma Dad I sez, "Five bob" (25 pence, an apprentice's starting wage) An' me Dad sez "No." I wis the eldest o' a big family an' there wis only one workin' besides ma Dad. So, I sez t' ma Dad, "Forget it, it doesna matter." Well, when I wis aboot sixteen an' a half the foreman plater cam t' me an' he sez, "What aboot servin' yer time as a plater?" I sez, "But I want t' be a Battle o' Britain pilot." He sez, "Forget yer hair brained ideas." I said, "I'll be a bomber pilot then." He sez, "Y' won't be nothin', you're in a reserved occupation go up t' office! I want y' t' sign the apprentices' book." You had to sign for indentures y' see. "But I'm not an apprentice." An' he sez, "I hevent told ya but I've had y' bloody name doon since y' were sixteen t' be a plater an' I've decided fer ya OK?" So that was that settled for me t' be a plater. So then I was approached to join the Boilermakers (Union) so I had t' go up to the branch t' get sworn in t' be a boilermaker and I'm still in the union. I'll always be a boilermaker.

Trevor: Did the director of Hall Russells come to the yard to inspect it and such like?

Walter: I wis in awe of onybody with rank, I'll be quite honest but I changed later on. I can tell ya a story about Hall Russells, a Mister Wilson, who owned the yard, a little dapper man he used t' come doon in his chauffeur driven Rolls Royce. Periodically he'd walk round the ship with management, foreman all the way doon the line. I was standin' on the deck rivetin' somethin' and the heater boy threw me a rivet and o' course y' wore big tackety boots in those days with studs in them y'know, As a rivet came towards me, I tried t' trap it y'know, I missed it an' it went into the turn up of Mr. Wilson's trousers. You can

The 2450 ton 'Sir Joseph Swan' about to take to the water in 1945. This was a special coaster built by Hall Russell and Co., it had a folding funnel and masts that telescoped to negotiate bridges on the Thames

imagine Trevor, I was terrified. I stood there and looked an' I could see it smoulderin'. I think I was frozen with fear 'cause t' me that was God. So, when the foreman bent doon an' got rid o' the rivet I never moved. Well he cam over an' he patted me on the head and he said t' me, "It's alright little boy I've got more trousers at home. Don't worry." I couldn't get home quick enough t' tell ma Dad! "The boss spoke t' me!" That was the attitude, You belong there and they belong there and ne'er the two shall meet.

Trevor: What about women workers?

Walter: Y' grew up in a very male oriented industry. Any feminist (sic) comin' near a ship wouldn't last five minutes. Well the war was on an' they brought women in the ship yard. I was terrified. I was a bit naïve an' I blushed terribly.

Trevor: Why, what did they do?

A selection of tools used in shipbuilding

Walter: They tormented me an' said risqué things in front of me. Socially outside the yard I was a little boy. I didna drink, I didna smoke. An' a lota the women, I'm sure it was a set up, they waited till I cam in aboot an' one o' them would say that her husband was home from the army then they would start talkin' aboot all the sex detail, I could feel ma face goin' red an' they giggled, I was a target for em. An' I remember the foreman put this lady on wi me t' collect scrap iron an' a course all the lads were sayin' once she gets ya doon there she'll hae the troosers aff yer. I wis feart, an' I went up the tap o' the mast on top o' the wheel house, an' she followed me! She was a hard nut too. Some o' them were nice, though I thought the men did a better job.

Trevor: What jobs did the women do?

Walter: There were three men that used t' tidy up the ship when it wis finished. Hand it over y' know clean it an' that. It would be forty women t' do the same job. I wouldn't say they did the same job but the war effort they had t' take women. Some o' them were good. Some o' them used t' drive the cranes. There wis one in Russells she used t' heat the rivets an' her face wis always black, because yer face is black, an' she'd big danglin' earrings. She used t' come oot o' the yard, we'd no washing' facilities or nothin' like at, y' jist came oot as y' went in. She wis a damn good heater, some o' them were very good. We were told t' cool it, curb yer tongue, Y' couldna imagine a shipyard, "I've jolly well bashed my finger!" We just don't say that. Well, we did curb out tongues but some o' the women were so hard that the men were gettin' embarrassed wi 'em. There were hard nuts. What I didna like aboot em was, they used t' come doon in the mornin' wi their bairn an' bung em intae York Street nursery. At night they'd meet a lad an' go t' the Neptune Bar, I thought that was wrong for a mum y'know. They made good money but they were a bloody nuisance, they were a pest on the Navy ships t' the sailors 'cause they got pickin's frae the sailors, cigarettes, sugar, and stuff y' couldna get outside or onythin'. I was given a job up the mast. I went up the mast an' lookit doon, there's a lifeboat swingin' outa the davits goin back an' fore. I nearly fell aff the mast, it wis this hard nut frae the Castle Hall Barracks! Boy, how y' finished yer education! When y' were young yer little ears would cock. See y' couldna start work till the blackout was lifted. So we used t' stand roond the furnace, we had the big furnaces in those days. The ribs o' the ship, they were put in straight. We'd t' pull it out white hot, shape it, set it, bevel it. It was hard work. Bloody hard work. You'd t' do a pair at a time y' see an' the furnace wis a meetin' point. Once daylight cam in y' could work. Y' could imagine a welder flashin' that weldin' plant a Jerry bomber could see it for miles away. One night we were workin' an' we had a tarpaulin ower it, there musta been a wee hole, the next minute, tat, tat, tat, tat, tat. A Jerry had come ower in the dark!

It finished up that I did ma apprenticeship from 1940 t' 1945.

Trevor: Could you tell me how you heated up the metal, as a plater what tools you used and how you used em.

ALEXANDER HALL & COMPANY, LIMITED.

ESTABLISHED 1790.

SHIPBUILDERS, ENGINEERS & BOILERMAKERS,

ABERDEEN.

ALL KINDS OF SHIP AND ENGINE
REPAIRS PROMPTLY EXECUTED.

COASTING STEAMERS, FISHING
VESSELS AND STEAM TUGS
A SPECIALITY.

OUR REF. ARW/MRH.

YOUR REF.

TELEPHONE No. 29121

TELEGRAMS-"HALL, ABERDEEN."

CODE-A.B.C. 5TH EDITION.

23rd August, 1951.

WALTER WATT,
7 Meadow Place, Woodside,
ABERDEEN.

We hereby certify that the above person
served his apprenticeship as a Shipyard Plater
from 25th November, 1940 to 24th November, 1945,
and from 8th March, 1948 to 1st June, 1951. He
also served in His Majesty's Forces from 16th
January, 1946 to 16th January, 1948.

During above periods we found him to be a
good tradesman and conscientious at his work, and
we can recommend him to anyone desiring his services.

He was paid off due to lack of work.

For ALEXANDER HALL & CO. LTD.

W.Y Smith Managing Director

Walter: The first things y' do is the ribs o' yer ship and the angle bar. You had a frame squad an' you'd big blocks wi holes in em full o' pegs an' pins an' 'dogs'. Well the first thing you'd do is, you'd have a set o' boards wi all the lines o' yer ship from the forepeak to the stern an' y' frame numbers start from the stern o' the ship, zero, then one, two, three, four, five the more numbers the longer the boat. Then you've y' decks, mid deck, boat deck. An' y' start wi the ribs an' what y' do is ya put em in the furnace an' shape em and bevel em.

Trevor: How did y' handle them when they were hot?

Walter: You'd put on a hook on a chain and y' pulled the plate onto the floor white hot. You poked em about wi the end o' yer hammer, y' already had a set in the ground, cold, to whatever shape it was, then y' got a hydraulic ram put a pin behind it. Then y' squeezed the plate in. Then y' hid t' get a whees(?) That's the thing for opening up an'

Above: Walter's letter of recommendation from A. Hall & Co. - 1951
Left: Larking about for the camera

yer had an anchor, it wis shaped like an anchor, everything wis done on the blocks then y' wheesed it and pushed it, an' pushed it about. Y' had t' beat the heat remember.

Trevor: Were the blocks made of wood?

Walter: Oh no, heavy cast iron. Y' had t' work in heavy cast iron. It was amazing how pliable that steel plates was. There was a lotta plates y' could bend cold. I must tell you here, A. Hall and Company was the most antiquated shipyard in Great Britain. I was workin' wi machinery which originally was steam driven. An' durin' the war a shipyard inspector cam round. The foreman took him round the platin' department and the inspector said, "Mr. Walker, I've seen many antiquated yards in Britain but I never saw a yard like this!"

The aulder platers found it very difficult t' adapt t' weldin'. It wis either a bolt or a rivet. It wasna that weldin' was new but the design o' ships wis changin'. It made my trade easier, I could cut a bit aff an' stick a bit on y' couldna de at wi a rivet. There was a lot more skill wi a riveted ship an' y' were paid every hundred rivets an' ya had t' mak a thousand rivets a day t' mak money an' that's some going. I'll tell you, it was a very beautiful sight t' see a hand squad knockin' doon a rivet. Now I'm left handed so I wida been handy. Y' need a left hander an' a right hander and we were often handy for one side o' the ship compared t' a right hander. It was a lovely sight t' see em knock a rivet doon, comin' through white hot an' the way it spread oot under the hammers. Y' called it battin' a rivet. Now they'd splayed it down, then they'd g' back t' the one they jist did an' finish it. So the man inside, don't hear what your sayin' 'cause o' the noise, he knows that, he'd jist shift his shoulder knowin' what t' d' next. Y' didna only have the riveters y' had the caulkers as well which was the noisiest o' the lot. It was a pneumatic chisel, 2,000 times a minute and you're on the inside an' he's on the outside you don't know he's comin' t' do it.

Workmen remove the wedges in preparation for the launch of the 'Empire Fenchurch' - 1945

Suddenly, yer brain goes blank, yer stone deaf wi the noise. Industrial deafness was a hazard. We'd got two deaths, they died from industrial deafness, it didna stop at the ear it went straight into the brain. No, there's a lot more in it than jist a ship. It's nice t' see them slidin' intae the water. I wish I'd a pound for every one I've seen. I remember the corvette the Hyderbad an' Lord and Lady Embray came t' the shipyard t' launch the ship. For the first time, there were Movietone news cameras there, and I was fascinated with it. Everything wis goin' fine, he christened it wi the champagne. Bang! She started t' move and suddenly she slipped right on her side. She took down stagin,' air pipes an' cables an' a' thing. She hit the water alright but she took a bit o' a list. That's the head foreman's job, y' can imagine, he's shoutin' fer everybody t' get t' the other side o' the ship. Well I don't know but that ship was a Jonah. A chap died in the tanks, we had a hell o' a job gettin' him out. We couldna get him out, we were in bowels o' the ship. You'd give a rattle on the side o' the ship to let them know it was finishin' time, nobody carried watches in those days. Well he didn't show up and when we found him he was dead. We couldn't get him out so we sez t' the managers "We'll hae t' tek off a shell plate t' get him out between the ribs." "Ye can't dee 'at!" We had to in the end cause there wis nae other way. He'd got jammed doon there be the propeller an' the doctor came down wi a nurse an' sez, "You'll hae t' break his legs t' get him oot". We werna goin' t' dee at so we took off the plate. I've seen some bad accidents, there wis an engineer screamin' one day. We were liftin' a propeller to swing it in line wi the shaft an' the lugs that held the gear, one o' em broke an' swish, sliced off his leg. Oh yea, I've seen a few dead in ma time.

H.M.S. CAREFUL LAUNCHED

YOUNG shipyard workers crowded the deck of the Admiralty naval tug, H.M.S. Careful, as she slid down the slipways at the launching ceremony at Messrs Alexander Hall & Co. Ltd.'s yard last week. The naming ceremony was performed by Mrs W. F. Dodd, wife of the Admiralty Ship Overseer for Aberdeen.

Top: No.2 bay Hall Russells
Above: Young shipyard workers crowd the bow of H.M.S. Careful at the launch

As a shipyard worker y' belonged to a race on yer own.

Trevor: A bit like the miners then?

Walter: Yes, an' even if y' go on yer holidays an' yer meet a man from anither shipyard whether he's a Geordie, or frae Glasgow or what, you'd something in common. We're a race o' wi own, we've a rough sense o' humour and we'd a way of life. They worked hard they played hard an' they never made a lotta money and when I look back there was no pressure you'd never heard o' heart attacks that y' get t' day.

THE PAPER INDUSTRY

The paper industry in Aberdeen still plays a significant economic role with two paper mills working. The paper industry emerged in the 1750's with the Culter Paper Mills which was later taken over by Alex Pirie and Company of Stoneywood which more recently amalgamated with Guardbridge Paper Company of Fife then shortly closing down in 1981. This was the last of paper making on the Dee. In 1770 a paper mill was set up at Stoneywood on the Don also run by Alexander Pirie which was later amalgamated by Wiggins Teape and Company. At about the same time, a paper mill downstream from the Stoneywood mill was set up at Mugiemoss the production of which was maintained by C. Davidson and Company until it was acquired by British Plaster Board LTD., although still operating under its former name.

Above: S.S. Linda arrives in Aberdeen with a cargo of Esparato grass
Centre: Newspaper cutting showing newsprint making at Donside Paper Mills
Below: Secret Wartime work for the paper mills. Thirteen hundred five ton turrets for Churchill Tanks were machined and finished at Stoneywood.

Andy Lawson: The buildin' that the cuttin' machines were in was massive, there were thirteen cuttin' machines, an' there wis about eight calender machines, there wis balkers, there wis slittin' machines. The conditions at that particular time were pretty cold.

David Moir: There were two extremes if I can interrupt there, because the makin' department was very hot 'cause you needed a lot o' heat to evaporate the water outa the paper but when it moved up t' the finishing end where Andy worked it tended t' be a lot colder.

Andy: Well different managers came t' the mill an' they always had something that was to be changed. Because I remember at one particular time it was no smoking in the mill an' that was a thing that I took a very, very grim view of. They used t' take the doors aff the toilets so if the folk went into the toilet t' have a smoke y' could easily get caught an' it could be really embarrassin'.

David Moir: It was also instant dismissal—

Andy: There wis one particular toilet there, an' it wis jist a pipe an' there wis six seats wi jist the pot-holes an' there wis a tank o' water an' that flushed it. There wis a urinal here an' it run doon past yer feet. But that particular door, that was taken aff too. This other toilets that I'm

Top: A girl worker drills a Churchill Tank turret at Stoneywood Mills
Centre: Newspaper cutting on Donside Paper Mills
Below: Unloading paper pulp at Aberdeen Harbour

spikin' aboot, y' coulda been seen from the outside there an' that was one thing that I took a very dim view of an' I got the doors back on. Smoking wis still prohibited but then a different manager cam on and I was the Union representative at that particular time and he enjoyed a smoke so I approached him an' I sez til him, "D' y' think it wid be a good idea t' introduce smokin' squares in the department?", folk were smokin' in all sorts o' places some o' them were dangerous places. There wis lots o' paper aboot and in the rag sortin' department y' were liable t' spontaneous combustion with the dust an' a' that. So, I sez to this particular manager I sez, "What about introducin' smoke squares where people can enjoy a smoke without the fear a bein' caught or creatin' a danger o' fire?"

David Moir: Everybody was under the impression that if smokin' was allowed the insurance would go up but in fact when it was allowed the insurance came down because it wis more under control.

Andy: Well the manager said t' me, "I can't understand why y' haven't asked me this before, I could go oot now an' walk roond the mill an' I would catch at least forty five people smokin', I know where they smoke I did it m'self." So we got smokin' squares introduced.

Woman: I left school at 14 and my first job was at Pirie Appleton's paper factory. It was at the bridge in Guild Street.

The hooter rang at ten minutes to eight and five minutes to eight every morning and by the time the last hooter stopped, if you were at the top of the avenue when the last hooter went you had to flee down and get stamped in at the clock before eight.

Above: **The 'Salle' or paper sorting room at the Stoneywood mill of Alex. Pirie and Sons Ltd.**

There were about six departments, starting from the cotton. There was the cutting department then the gumming. Third was the machine room where the envelopes were made. The fourth department was the stock room whilst the fifth was the box room where the boxes were made for the envelopes. The sixth department was the hand folding where I worked. I was like a messenger. I took samples down to other departments. There were six of us, all starting together. We had all just left school. We had to supply the hand folders who were on piece work with boxes for their envelopes.

After about three months I was taught how to hand fold. I got a pack of paper all cut and shaped, with a white bone, shaped like a pallet knife. We had to make sure we hadn't any holes showing at the corners. And all our work was examined. We had a mistress, Nan Burnett and an under mistress, Myma Cooper. They were a bit strict. The only thing I remember was on a pay day we all went around swapping our sweets with one another. I got 7/6 (37.5p) wages in old money but when I went on to piece work I made 15 shillings (75p), which was a lot of money at that time 58 years ago. I only stayed there one and a half years then I got a job in the Sixty Minute Cleaners in Union Street. My two daughters both worked there when they left school.

Maureen worked there for ten years and then she left to get married but Evelyn just stuck it for one year.

Pirie Appleton was closed down in the '60's and they had a new factory built at Dyce which came under the name of Wiggins Teape Stationery. Another thing I remember was I used to run home after dinner time to hear Henry Hall's Dance Band with Betty Driver. She was a good singer and she was my pin up girl at the time. She is now Betty Turpin on Coronation Street.

COMBS

The Aberdeen Combworks Company Ltd. was the oldest comb making firm in Britain having been in existence for over 140 years. The basic material used for making combs in the early days was horn. Early in the 20th century they produced their own non-inflammable plastic material from casein. Keronyx, as it was called, was available in an infinite variety of colours. In 1937 the company installed an injection moulding plant from which highly finished combs, and other domestic goods such as egg cups, egg spoons, bathroom tiles and cutlery trays were produced under the trade name of Nuroid.

In 1963 the Aberdeen Comb works amalgamated with Montgomery's of Glasgow. Unfortunately, the comb works was burned down in April 1969.

Alice Black: I worked in the comb works for two and a half years. The bone just lay everywhere it was filthy. The bone had t' be soaked in boilin' water for hours before they could be used so y' were workin' ahead all the time. There would be about eighteen machines an' you'd be workin' on and on and on.

David: Did the bone come off in squares then?

Alice: Yes dependin' on the size o' the tooth combs you were doin'. There were big ones and small ones an' y' worked em two at a time y'ken. The machine that you worked - y' put two on each one. That wis one machine an' y' fixed em so that the saws went in and made the teeth, the saws went in an' did the teeth then y' turned em and did the other side. They were twin edged comb -.

David: Bean combs?

Alice: Yes, bean combs that's what they were called. But it was filthy and it was a horrible smell. When I used t' go home at tea time ma sisters an' ma mither would smell me when I went in an' they'd say "What a terrible smell!" It was at the outbreak of war when I went into the comb.

David: What put you off?

Alice: It was too claustrophobic an' I had worked in the fish an' I got fresh air all the time in the fish.

David: So you preferred working in the fish then?

Alice: Oh yes and it's a lot healthier an' er - a feelin' o' freedom.

Mary Milne: I worked in the comb works in Hutcheon Street. I started at fourteen and was there for eight years. A lotta things surprised me for example the bosses were

Above: A spectacular blaze at Aberdeen Combworks in April 1969 (photo courtesy of Aberdeen Journals)

very harsh. I was caught one day doing my work and eating my morning roll at the same time. There was no breaks in them days so I'm eating my morning roll and the manager cam in, aye the works manager. He never spoke t' me but he mentioned it t' the gaffer. The gaffer cam in about t' me an' he said t' me, "Dinna eat y' roll fen he comes in about. He dinna want t' see it." To which my mistress turned round an' said, "Hu! I remember, he didna sit an eat rolls he wis sittin' drinkin' whisky!" An' she sez, "I think that's a lot worse than eatin' a roll." I really was, no, I'm bein' honest, I was carryin' on doin' my work. Which was a very monotonous job. I was in the, what they called the 'ending department'. The combs were all made with machinery. Now we did have the horn work which was all done by hand but by this time, plastic, well it wasn't plastic it was 'onyx' an' things like that. Well, y' poured this stuff into the machine, pressed a few buttons an' out came four combs all joined together. It was all done very quick you understand. So, as the combs were broken up, put into boxes, we had to smooth off the ends. So, it was called the endin'. Comb work was considered very important at the time. I'm going by what I hear, it was the only comb work that was workin' in Britain the rest had been bombed. Now at that time I really wanted t' get into the shipyard and I would have liked to have done welding but I couldn't get out of the comb works because it was the only comb work that was working in Britain. So, I was stuck in the comb works

Advert for Aberdeen Comb Works

doing a very monotonous job and I thought that my brain was equipped t' do something better! Of course the fact of it was, I always made good money.

David: What other jobs did the comb works have if the original manual jobs were done by machinery?

Mary: Well, everything wasn't done by machinery some was done by hand. The combs had t' be put into boxes naturally, an' all this sorta thing but a lot of the work that was done by hand was; the combs had t' be polished, the points had t' be put on to the combs. Beatrice and Margaret, her sister, worked in a department which they called the 'scorin' shop'. They all had t' be scored before that t' get them all up to a fine point y'know.

That sorta took the roughness off them, then they were pointed then they were put up t' this place that we called the 'buff shop' where they were polished. They were polished on big buffs that went round made of cloth. Then there was the fine work like egg spoons. That was horn, egg spoons and shoe horns that was what they considered fine work and maybe a specialised person would have done that. They also made ornaments with the horn that came off. I've seen sails on a ship made from part of the horn and things like that but there was an enormous amounts of combs made. The ones that were made from 'onyx', that machines that were workin' on shifts, eight hour shifts. Two till ten, ten till six, six till two. There were maybe three or four big machines in that machine shop, they were turning out a terrific amount of 'onyx' combs. We also turned out the proverbial bone comb (for head lice) fer doin' the hair. Would y' like t' know what we called em?

David: Bean combs?

Mary: Ah, but we'd anither name - louse trappers! Ha, ha, ha!

ENGINEERING

Aberdeen's engineering industry by the 1950's had grown to considerable proportions with the industry employing roughly 7000 people. The need of other industries for specialised equipment promoted this growth in particular in the granite, paper and shipbuilding industries. The demands of agriculture for the continuing evolution of farm machinery was also instrumental in the growth of engineering.

Not withstanding the local demand in Aberdeen for engineering goods the industry had markets world wide. For example, McKinnon's, in Spring Garden near the Gallowgate had manufactured machinery for the coffee industry since 1798 and later found a demand for rice milling machinery. Their connections were world wide wherever coffee and rice were grown.

The firm John M. Henderson & Co. Ltd. Kings Works provided a variety of handling equipment often in response to the initial needs of the granite industry and thereafter re-applied their designs to suit the requirements of many other industries world wide (such as cranes for the Forth Road Bridge). Besides Henderson's and McKinnon's there were other firms involved in engineering, many were small but others, for example Barry Henry and Cook and C.F. Wilson were of considerable size.

Jim Gauld: I started working for McKinnon's in 1937 at the age of fifteen and my idea was after I had served my time was t' go out t' Malaya t' Kuala Lumpur I had a friend who worked at 'Jacks' out there an' I was goin' out t' work wi him but unfortunately the war came about an' that was finished. Anyway the wages at that time at McKinnon's was four and eight pence a week that's like aboot 23 pence. I used t' travel from Stoneywood to Hutcheon Street by the suburban train which cost me ten shillin's a month so ma mother had t' subsidise me really. It improved durin' the first year o' the war, the apprentices in Clydeside went out on strike in 1940 or 41 and the wages jumped by a pound a week across the whole o' Scotland. My time wis out in '42 and the wages were about two pounds five shillings or something like that. The funny thing about it was we were makin' fourteen pound a week bonus wi the production o' shells and the containers o' gas that went into the nose o' the shells. I discovered that these firms got paid by the government costs plus ten percent. The total bill for rates, everything plus ten percent so the more they paid the workers the more the management got for themselves.

David: Could you describe a normal days work?

Jim: I'd get up about half past six with a struggle. The normal breakfast would be porridge and sometimes you got a piece o' bread and jam. Then I went up t' Stoneywood station and got the suburban train t' Hutcheon street. Then t' McKinnon's at Spring Garden, inta the lodge. You'd a check, 124 I think was my number an' there was three slots. One, if you were on time, you put it in. When the hooter went the lodge keeper closed that slot so the next slot showed that you'd a quarter o' an hour off your wages then efter a quarter of an hour that slot was closed and you were half an hour late an' after that y' didna get in. I started in what was known as the pipe shop an' I wis pit on t' the mechanical saw t' saw off all the material. Round bar, angle iron, an' you were on that saw till the next apprentice started. Y' got tickets for all the materials from the different departments an' you had t' saw it a' off. The saw was belt driven from a gas engine. They made their own gas from coke (coal?). All the machinery was driven by belts. The boiler shop floor was made o' sand an' I remember we made big tanks for the soap place, Ogstons in Loch Street. We used t' heat the rivets and hold em on and used the big hammer an' that. In the pipe shop that was a cement floor then down in the main shop there was a gallery upstairs wi a wooden floor. There was a lotta machinery up in the gallery. Well, I was in the pipe shop for about three months. From there I went on t' making catadoors, they still make then t' this day. It takes the beans up in a bucket on a chain which takes the coffee beans up t' distributes them to the next process which might be gradin' somethin' like that. I think there are about six processes for a coffee bean.

Everything we made, castings, the lot was made at McKinnon's. There was a big pattren shop where we made a' the pattrens.

David: It must have been quite strange for you to have women working in the engineering works during the war. How did it feel to suddenly have that?

Above: Interior of Wm. McKinnon & Co. Ltd. Spring Garden, Aberdeen

Jim: Well it seemed to give us all a lift. Instead o' arguin' wi each other we had other things t' do, go out at nights an' things like that. I'll be quite honest the two years that I was at McKinnon's, I was taken out in 1943 and taken to Fraserburgh, from 1941 to 1943, it's a terrible thing t' say but they were the best two years o' my life! That was because o' the mixed company. There was a hundred an' eighty one girls worked at McKinnon's and there were about fifty men at that time. They were all types, fish, banks, offices, shops - they were a mixed lot. They were directed into the forces so they came into the munitions here at McKinnon's.

At that time I was a setter. I set the tools for the machine operator. You sharpened the tool, the drill or whatever was required. There was a threadin' machine that put a thread on the job, it was primitive compared with t'day.

There was another chap on wi me, we did alternative fortnights, I did a fortnight day shift, he'd a fortnight night shift.

The inspecting girls, they were government employed they inspected a' the jobs. Well, there were a lot o' them an' we used t' have a lark. This night they came efter me an' got a hold o' me by ma tie. I passed out, they'd choked me with my tie. O, they were panicked, the girls couldna do enough for me efter that!

Above: Items produced by McKinnons -
Top: 'B' Pulper with shaking sieve
Bottom: 'X' size Madagascar Pulper

Skylarkin' landed me in hospital. I was on turnin' shells before I got on this job an' I was skylarkin' with another apprentice and I'd lifted this a hundred and forty odd pound rough castin' and I was goin' throw it at this chap but I turned roun' an' put it back in the bogey an' this chap shouted, "Watch yersel!" I henna pit it on properly an' it fell right on t' ma toes. Bruce Thomson took me up t' Foresterhill and I was off for six months wi plaster up t' here. They saved a' ma toes, the only thing that's missin' is that I'll never have a nail on ma big toe.

John Londragan: I lived recht opposite James Henderson's, ye know in West North Street - engineering works. And, they had a steam hammer and it <u>was</u> a steam hammer! A great big twenty ton steam hammer! Something like that ye know and it used to go 'Ooo' up, the noise up and down it come again, and we'd be lying in bed again and tossin' about like this. And we thought nothin' of it we got accustomed to it. And this went on all night. And just speakin' about overtime, do you know this, the word 'overtime' wasn't in the working class dictionary until about 1937 ... no such thing, you did the job. Here, there as the case may be that was required there was no overtime paid or anything like that. Either you did the job, got out or someone else'll take your place. No, it was as straight forward as that.

David: When did you start as an engineer?

George Cruickshank: I wasn't actually an engineer, I was a pattern maker. I wis the fella that made the machinery in wood and it then went to the

Top: A J.M. Henderson built crane at work on the Fraserburgh harbour extensions - c. 1890
Bottom: J.M. Henderson, Kings Works, King Street - the East Shop - c.1950

foundry where it was moulded and cast in metal, but the end product, the drawing office sent us the drawings, we made the patterns and then the castings went to the machine shop where they were machined and everything wis a' put t'gether.

David: When was this then, roughly; what years are we talking about?

George: Forty-nine, fifty I started.

David: What was the factory like?

George: Some bits were better than others, some parts of the workshop were done in cassies.

David: That was better?

George: Better than the earth floor.

David: What powered the machines?

Man: The machines were powered by the big gas engine away at the bottom o' the workshop which drove a series of shafts up the whole length o' the workshops.

David: What kept you warm in winter?

George: Eh coke stoves, cinder fires.

David: Where were they situated?

George: Well, there might have been half a dozen in the main enginery. We in the pattern shop had simply a hot village stove aboot so high with a chimney that gid oot through the corrugated iron roof.

David: So there was nothing between the corrugated iron and the outside.

George: No, just the dust n' the sawdust o' many, many moons.

David: What sort of wood did you make the patterns out of?

George: Usually Yellow Pine, sometimes Mahogany, depending what it was going to be but mainly Yellow Pine which once it was finished and got the okay off the gaffer. You painted it or varnished it dependin' on what it was.

It was then sent to one of the Aberdeen foundries. We dealt with Abernethy at the old chain bridge there, which is now a coal store. Thompson Stewart's in King Street, McArthur's brass foundry which is still on the go -they cast brass, aluminium and things like that. McKinnon's used t' have a foundry as well but they are now into a small workshop place. They were at the end of Gerrard Street in Spring Garden.

The building was made of three-quarter weather boarding. In the Winter it was damn cold with jist a corrugated iron roof an' as I say we had this one pot-bellied stove in the middle o' the floor but when drawings came down from the drawing office, there was only three of us at the very most in the pattern shop. We kept our own stock of Yellow Pine an' whatnot on the ground floor of the pattern shop and the machinery was all upstairs; circular saws, band saws turnin' lathe things like that. Y' just went about doin' the project given to you by the foreman and when you were finished you informed him, it might have taken you a week, it might have taken y' six weeks or six months dependin' on the size o' the job.

David: What sort of things did you make?

George: It was all parts of compressors, parts of stone workin' machinery, saws, Jenny Linds for polishing.

Norman Miller: Tell me, once the castin' wis made did it come back to your place?

George: Aye it cam back t' the engineerin' works.

Norman Miller: So it wis a pattern shop and a machine shop?

George: Oh yes, aye it was a drawin' office, a pattern shop and a machine shop. The patterns went to the foundry and then the castings came back.

David: If it was your pattern were you in control of making sure that the final piece was finished correctly?

George: No, we had t' produce the pattern which had an allowance on it for machining, boring and contraction. The rule that you used to make the pattern depended on the material because there was different contraction for cast iron, aluminium and brass so y' had t' use the right edge o' the rule for makin' the pattern.

Norman Miller: Did the patterns come back?

George: Yes, we had a huge pattern loft full of patterns from the First World War time. Sometimes you got firms all over the world sendin' back in for new bush bearings or parts of a machine

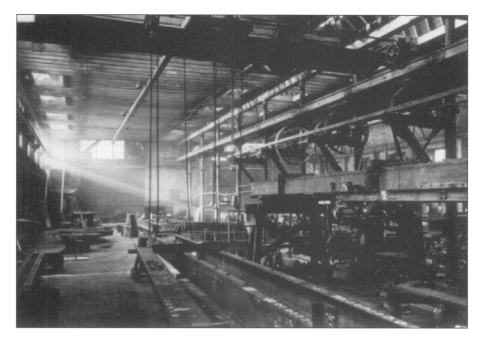

Above: Interior photographs of J.M. Henderson, Engineering Shop - c.1890

that had been broken. So we'd a big pattern shed jist like the shipyards and any engineering works.

Peter Rennie: Look at the farm implements like a the binder or a mower or onything like that, horse implements. All these were cast an' up until the war the blacksmith had no welding equipment and every time we broke a binder blade or onything like that it had t' go right back and y' had t' get a part number. The blacksmith sent away for it but then durin the war they startit this auld fashioned gas welding and so they welded the two bits together, sometimes three bits. If the horse ran aff wi the mower or the horse ran aff wi the binder an' something hut something like a wall an' perhaps stripped a' the cogs o' the wheels.

Top: Wm. McKinnon & Co. Ltd. - last casting at the works - 15th October 1992
Bottom: Workers at the last casting

David to George: Did you ever do any work for farm implements or was it always granite?

George: No, no it was nearly all for the granite trade. All these road compressors that you see goin' around being towed behind lorries, great big things some o' them, we made these things as well for the road makers and the quarries for the likes of Rubislaw an' that. There was a lot o' Wilson's compressors around there.

Woman: Did they get paid well in the foundry?

George: No, naebody was well paid at that time, it wasnae until y' got into the late '50's intae '60's before pay became reasonable.
   When I went there first t' Wilson's in Ashgrove Road, it was in the stores as a store boy it was sixteen an' six a week an' then when I started ma time it went up to a pound and a *tanner or something like that. The last year (of the apprenticeship) I got up to five pounds.

A tanner was six old pence or 2.5 new pence.

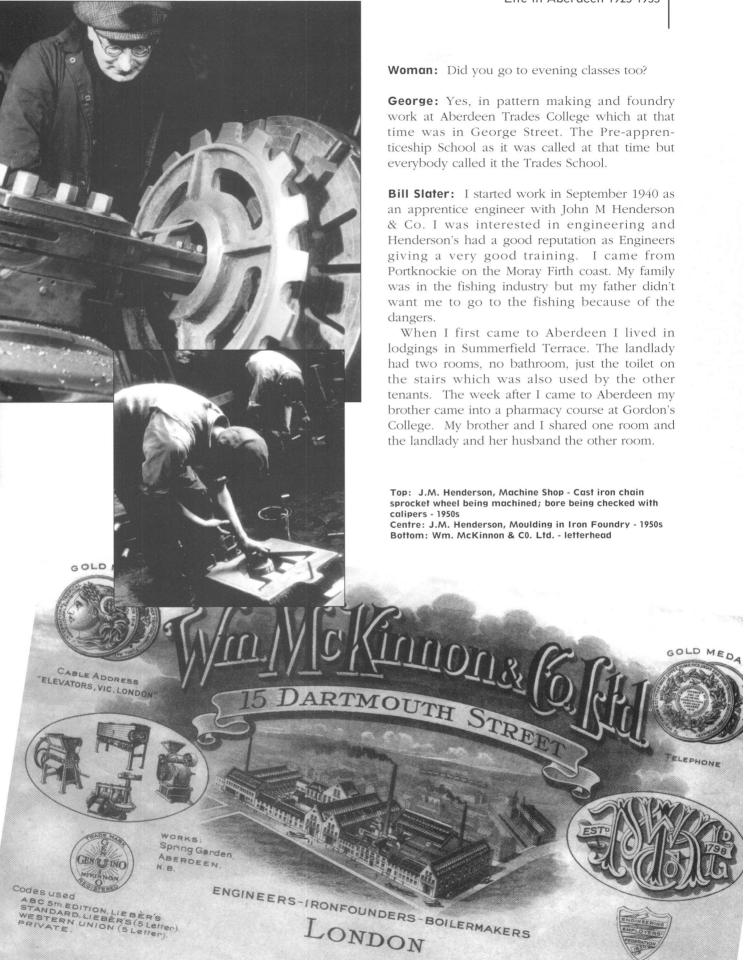

Woman: Did you go to evening classes too?

George: Yes, in pattern making and foundry work at Aberdeen Trades College which at that time was in George Street. The Pre-apprenticeship School as it was called at that time but everybody called it the Trades School.

Bill Slater: I started work in September 1940 as an apprentice engineer with John M Henderson & Co. I was interested in engineering and Henderson's had a good reputation as Engineers giving a very good training. I came from Portknockie on the Moray Firth coast. My family was in the fishing industry but my father didn't want me to go to the fishing because of the dangers.

When I first came to Aberdeen I lived in lodgings in Summerfield Terrace. The landlady had two rooms, no bathroom, just the toilet on the stairs which was also used by the other tenants. The week after I came to Aberdeen my brother came into a pharmacy course at Gordon's College. My brother and I shared one room and the landlady and her husband the other room.

Top: J.M. Henderson, Machine Shop - Cast iron chain sprocket wheel being machined; bore being checked with calipers - 1950s
Centre: J.M. Henderson, Moulding in Iron Foundry - 1950s
Bottom: Wm. McKinnon & C0. Ltd. - letterhead

David: When did you start work then?

Bill: I came in on the September holiday weekend which was a Monday, started work on the Tuesday and attended engineering classes at Robert Gordon's College three nights a week.

My first impression coming into the Henderson's Works was that it was a massive place, at that time Henderson's employed about 700 people.

I started off in the machine shop where there were slotting, shaping, milling and turning machines.

There was one job I remember in particular in the early days. After the sinking of the Royal Oak at Scapa Flow, Winston Churchill gave orders to build what is now known as the Churchill Causeways. Aerial Cableways, a Henderson speciality, were required for the building but such was the urgency they could not wait for new machines to be built and Henderson's sent an Engineer to the Middle East to inspect the Henderson cableways which had just completed the building of a barrage. These were shipped to Aberdeen, modernised and re-erected at Scapa. My small part as a first year apprentice was cutting keyways in a large number of pulleys, not knowing at that time what they were to be used for. Later I gained experience in various parts of the machine and fitting shops.

We started work before 8am and the normal working week was forty-four hours with a lot of overtime during the war years. At that time there was a five year apprenticeship and after my third year I had the opportunity to move up to the drawing and estimating offices, but then you had to pay for the privilege of getting off the shop floor by having your apprenticeship extended from five to six years. Later I became the Sales Manager and then the General Manager.

Our speciality was mechanical handling plant, including cranes and aerial cableways. As shown in the brochure we made cranes for the sugar industry in Jamaica.

David: How did Aberdeen get involved in making things for the sugar industry in Jamaica and the coffee and tea industry in other parts of the world? What was the connection between Aberdeen and these far flung countries?

A selection of metal castings from the streets and pavements of Aberdeen, showing the foundries where each was cast.

Top: Machine Shop - Barry, Henry and Cook, 1914-18
Bottom: Coal Bagger produced by Barry, Henry and Cook

Bill: Engineering companies in Aberdeen always trained a lot of engineers and many, after completing their apprenticeship, went abroad to the sugar states, the tea states or the coffee growing countries. They never forgot the companies at home and in many cases were responsible for orders being placed in the UK.

The first time I went abroad was in 1948 when we were building a big dam in Portugal after the war. Henderson had four aerial cableways and six draglin excavators which were used for excavating the sand and gravel from the bed of the river.

David: Where did you build your suspension bridges?

Bill: Mainly in Nepal but that was in the 1920's and the 1930's. They were very small suspension bridges.

David: What did Henderson make during the war? (Second World War)

Bill: 4.5 Gun Carriages, ammunition hoists, winches, cranes, electric furnaces, heavy cargo blocks and general mechanical handling plant.

FARMING

Farming in Aberdeenshire was and continues to be a widespread occupation albeit with an immensely reduced workforce due to mechanisation. The production of beef, notably the 'Aberdeen Angus' gave prominence to the agriculture of Aberdeenshire country wide. The production of barley, for beef stock feeding and for malting, remains a major cereal crop in the North East. Potatoes, particularly for seed has been a crop in demand by the South and latterly the European continent. Although not an industry directly relating to the centre of Aberdeen, its importance regarding food stuffs and the feeding of a large city was considerable and at that time, before the creation of its suburbs, Aberdeen was but a half mile radius with agriculture on its periphery.

Peter Rennie: Fin I wis fourteen year aul, a wis ta'en awa fae the squeel, an I hid t' start at fee't life. The feein aye startit wi the feein' markets. At wis far the fairmers an' the fairm servants got agither t' thrash oot the wages, or the fees as they caaed em. The feein' markets wis far the servants bargained themselves intae their neest sax months wark, till the neest term. The feein' markets were held in the market toons o' the country o' Aiberdeenshire. They were held the week before the term days. The term days war aye the 28th o' May an' the 28th day o' November. A feein' market wis held here in Aiberdeen doon in the Castlegate the side nearest the sea. It wis held the Friday afore the term an' wis caed the Muckle Friday. An unofficial feein market wis held in the same place, the Friday efter the term. It wis caed Rascal Friday cis at wis faar the loons gaed at hid runawa fae their places. A coorse they took their wiks wages !

("Muckle Friday" in the Castlegate, Aberdeen. — Left: Major M'Donald recruiting officer, Depot Gordon Highlanders, gives the farm "loons" a talk on the benefits of joining the Army. Above: "Fit wid ye be seekin'?"—an actual feeing in progress. ("P. and J." Copyright.)

Top: Three horses pulling a binder?
Centre: 'Muckle Friday' in the Castlegate, Aberdeen. An actual feeing in progress.
Bottom: Major McDonald recruiting officer, Depot Gordon Highlanders, gives the farm loons a talk on the benefits of joining the army.

John Londragan: And where we are here now, Castle Hill, this used to be the barracks, the Gordon's barracks this is where we are and down below is the parade ground where the soldiers used to drill and all the rest o' it. Just off Market Street, Hadden Street it was, there was a small square, it was here that the farmers was comin' in every six months and hired the hands for the farming an' so forth 'cause the farm servants signed up for a term, a term was usually about six months. They'd come in beforehand and they'd give 'em about five bob and this was the contract for the rest of the term. Also, at that time, the colour sergeants from the Gordon's would be down there tryin' to recruit the lads for the army. They'd give 'em a shillin', the King's shillin', they'd give 'em a shillin' to join the army. A number o' lads who'd worked on the farms for quite some time, had got fed up o' it would take a shillin' and join the army. All this was going on at the same time, all this sort o' thing.

Peter Rennie: A aye mysel gied ti Ellon feein market. It wis held the Tuesday before the term. It wis held in Market Street in Ellon, atween the aul brig an the New Inn closs. On the Market day the pavement o' the street nearest the Ythan wis happit wi' stalls. The eyin een nearest the brig wis aye taen bi a man as a sheetin stall. He aye hid a habit o' sayin 'It's a wee kittie heich, high, low, an' laich'. The een stall nearest the New Inn wis taen bi chaip Johns sellin sic like trock as collar studs an tiepreens, razor blades an' butterflee brooches. They selt tins o' strong smellin brilliantine. Fan the loons eest t' pit it on t' their hair i' the Simmer time they eest ti be bothert wi the flees! The chaip Johns selt three an ninepenny pocket watches wi' a pictir o a railway engine on the face o them. They caad the watches the railway time keepers, bit the watches usually jist gaed for aboot a fortnicht, syne stoppit.

Forbye the stall keepers there wir aye salesmen stottin aboot. A man gaed roon wi' a wyin machine an he eest t' guess yer wecht. Anither man gaed aboot wi' a contraption wi' a clock faced dial on't. Fan ye steed on t' the machine an pood twa hanles on the tap o' the machine, the han on the dial gied roon. He eest ti say 'See how strong the body is, he needs no cod liver oil in the mornings'. Anither man went roond sellin market candy in cardboard boxes. He eest ti shout 'Fred's candy, Fred's candy, six pence the half pound'. A man eest ti ging roon sellin pies made o mince. He used t' shout 'Hot pies! Hot pies two for tuppence!', Syne a minute efter, aneeth his breath, he said 'each'.

Fan a fermer got a haud o a loon, t' please him hid t' gie the loon his 'arles'. Fan the loon took the arles, usually aboot a shillin, at wis his promise at he wid bide at the ferm for sax months. At wis the length o' the term. At wis jist the same as the sodger takin the King's shillin. Spikin o sodgers, a pipe band o the Gordon's eest t' aye come oot ti Ellon feein market, fae their depot in Aiberdeen. They fell in at the Square an maischt doon ti the closs in front o the New Inn door. The recruitin sodgers war aye there pickin up ony ferm servants at hidna gotten a fee. There wis aye plenty o them cis there wir aye mair fairm servants than there were jobs for them it at time. The regular battalions o the Gordons hid a gweed curn fairm servants in them.

The fee'd life wis a hard life an the work wis lang an sair. The oors war fae sax o'clock i' the mornin ti sax at nicht sax days a week. Ower an abeen at oors the horse hid t' be cleant an fed an sortit on the Sundays. Ye got naethin for at. The horse hid aye t' be fed an watert at echt o'clock at nicht. The wages wir neen ower gweed either. A loon leavin the squeel at fourteen year aul wis gettin sax pown for sax months wark. The fee wis aye payt at the eyn o the term. Ye wis expect t' live on the arles the first sax month!

The fairm servants in Aiberdeenshire got fed i' the fairm kitchen an they slept i' the chaulmer. The chaulmer wis usually the laft abeen the stable neest the hay laft. The fee't loons eest t' be bothert wi the hay worms crawlin through the partition fae the hay laft in the winter time an they wir bothert wi' the blue mites i' the simmer time! They cam throw t' the heat o' the chaulmer. On some o' the bigger fairm toons the chaulmer wis a sma steen biggin set doon near the stable usually at the back o' the midden dyke. Inside the chaulmer wis biggit in twa timmer beds and cauf beds set on t' them. The kists the men keepit their belongings in war been the side o' the teem waa. The kists wae halt roon the chaulmer fire at nicht an the men sat doon on them. Things got a bittie better as the 30's gied on though. Thanks to a man caad Josey Duncan fa startit up the Fairm Servants Union. The fairm servants got a half day on a Setterday. We finished workin aboot een o'clock an the lave o' the day wis our ain inless, a coorse ye wasna catcher aboot the place. (The catcher wis the man at sortit aa the beasts aboot the place at the weekens, if it wis his turn.) Es half day leets nip doon the fairm road t' the road eyn an catch the bus t' Aiberdeen t' aa the sichts o' Airberdeen. The bus fare wisna muckle it at time cis there wis a price war atween the railways an Jamie Sutherlan' at aint the buses. We cam aff the bus at Mealmarket Street in Aiberdeen an held on up King Street the wye o the Castlegate. The toon's folk sa us comin a mile awa

an kent us fae the country. A suppose it wis the wye we dressed. Fyles ye wid hae some o' the toon loons shoutin 'Country Geordie!' i' oor backs, bit we niver leet on.

Fan we won the length o the Castlegate we micht jump on a tram an gang doon t' the sea beach. It wis a number five. Fan we got t' the beach, if we hid ony spare siller, we hid a hurl on the scenic railway. Sometimes we went intae the boxin booths. Some o the brozy fairm chiels took on the challenge o' the boxers. If they could laist three minutes against them they got 10/- bit maist o' them jist laistit till the first skelp!

If we didna ging t' the beach we fyles took a taik doon Marischal Street ti the hairber ti see fit wis daein there. Efter at we wid waak ben Union Street as far as Market Street. We aye stoppit at the heid o' Market Street t' get a look at the horses climbin the brae with their loads an the tracin horses in the front. The loons at caad the tracin horses were daab haans at lowsin oot the tracer horses fan they got on to the level bit o

Top: Two horses and farm loon.
Bottom: Outside view of Neils music shop with Mrs. Jolley in the foreground.

Union Street. They eest ti hae the horse heuchit an turnt roon an doon Market Street with oot ever devaalin. Nae traffic lichts at the crossin then t' bother aboot! Fyles ye micht a seen a bobby steppin oot t' the middle o' Union Street an haudin up a tram till the horse an his load got clear o' the tram lines!

We eest t' turn intae St. Nicholas Street, doon the neuk an ben the Netherkirkgate by the 'Mannie in the tower'. In some o' yon sma side streets aff o' the Kirkgate ye foun the street musicians the likes o' Curly McKay playin there. Fan we won the tap o' the street we crossed ower Broad Street tae the tap o' Queen Street. Near the een o' the street wis Neil's music shop. It wis faar we brocht oor gramophone records. Aa the local artists, the like o Harry Gordon, Curly Mckay, Geordie Morris, Willie Kemp an' Saffton Scott fae Inverurie eest tae record on Biltona records an the records cost us half a croon each oota Neil's shop.

Ye got a gweed mooth organ for 1s 6d. an a double keyt 'Little Lairdie' melodeon wisna ower dear t' buy. They wis caad 'Little Lairdie' bit they wis made in Germany!

Aside Neil's shop wis Mckay's second haan claes shop faar the fairm servants brocht some o' their workin claes. The shop assistants wir sich gweed salesmen they eest t' heuk the navy blue serge suits aff o' the back o' the shop door faar they eest t' hing, blaa the stew aff o' the suits an tellt us t' try on the jacket for size. 'A perfect fit laddie' they wid say an aa the time wid hae a hanfu o' the jacket i' their knieve!

We aye usually gied t' the Newmarket for oor tay. Upstairs i' the Newmarket wis faar the young ferm loons feenisht their education! We aye feenisht up wir trip tae Aiberdeen by gyan t' the education! syne on t' the bus an hame.

At the een o the '30's the war cam on an at feenisht aarthing as it wis. A wis callt up t' the army wi' me age group o twenty at the start o't an efter sax an a half year o't. A' wis richt gled t' see the green gress o' Aiberdeenshire again. A hid seen ower mony foreign countries an ower mony strange sichts.

Efter the war the feein markets wis a deen awa wi'. We hid t' live a different wye cis aathing wis different an I wis nae longer young an gypit!

Hirstin' in the 1930's. Note the traction engine providing power to the thrashing mill.

Adam Jack: Well it was long hours and very little pay. They were payin' men about thirty shillin's. There were some places that were payin' two shillin's more than that or two shillin's less as the case may be but women workers got maybe a pound a week and I reckon that they shoulda got the same as men 'cause there were lots o' jobs they could dae better than men an' they were doin' for two thirds the pay.

The foreman, he got a shillin' a week for knockin' on the doors at five o'clock for the men, he was on his road to the stable. I had a brother who didna get up till he knocked an' he used to come into the stable with his boots unlaced, even if he wis up in time he didna have them tied. It wis the last thing he did before he harnessed his horse.

David: Presumably if he just got up and went right out he didn't have time for shaving?

Adam: Oh he never shaved till the weekend unless he wis going somewhere! When I started wi' a horse, there wis four pair, five pair, and an odd horse. That's how you started, with an odd horse and then you moved up, maybe got the last pair. The first thing in the morning wis, the foreman, that was the man who knocked on the door, had a key for openin' the corn kist an' he had a scoop in there that wis a feed for each horse and ye had a bag, or two bags if you had two horses. So you filled each bag so that each horse had the same measure. That was jist the back o' five o'clock in the mornin'. Then you started cleanin' oot the straw and groom them and put in hay and anything that they needed. Then the grieve would come round an' tell you what you had got to do and you'd harness the horse(s) an' then at six o'clock the foreman would call 'bridal' an' you'd put the bridals on at that time. That place that I

worked at, the horses turned in the stall 'cause the stalls were fairly wide, they turned in their stall, come round an' got their bridal on but they'd already got their collar and their saddle on before that whichever you were goin' t' work with. The collars did for every job an' there wis iron hames used for cartin'. They fitted on the collar that the chains fitted on tae and on the plough harness y' had wooden hames which hadna the long fork on them and y' used these if y' wis workin' the plough or the harras.

I'll say now they'd land y' in the asylum for de'in what we did. We used t' go oot on a Sunday mornin' lookin' at ploughin' and lookin' at stacks comparin' them wi your own stacks. We took a pride in our work an' there was nothing else t' do. Y' work wis your main thing at that time.

Anyway, to get back to a typical day, dependin' what you were goin t' do, if you were goin cartin' y' had t' yolk it in to a cart an' go sometimes t' the station. Everything wis t' drive to and from the station at that time. Cattle cake, feedin' for sheep would come via the horse an' cart.

Top: Manufactured for Seaton Pottery by J. Lyon, blacksmith, Ashgrove Road, Aberdeen - closed 1985
Bottom: George R Lyon. Blacksmith.

David: If the weather was bad, if it was pouring with rain at six o'clock in the morning, you'd just go out and work normally?

Adam: Some places, — in the early part o' the winter like now, the sheep were fed on yellow turnips and they had sharse on them and o' course they were soakin' wet and at that time I canna remember anybody wearin' Wellington boots far less oilskins in fact y' had very little shoes a lot o' people only had tackety boots. Very few people had oilskins, what most of them had was a railway bag. The railways hired out bags for puttin' corn in. They held sixteen stone o' barley but they held eighteen stone o' wheat. When y' weighed them they were eighteen stone four pounds the four pounds was for the bag. They were made by prisoners in the jails an' we used t' snaffle one o' these an' put it roond yer shooders on a wet day. It was suprisin' how dry they could keep y'.

(For) Tatties there were a lot o' wee stations on the road at that time that only did farm work. They took in hundreds o' tons o' tatties for the London market.

After startin' at six o'clock, y' got a break at quarter past eight. Y' tea wis in a tin flask wi a bit o' brown paper wrapped roond it and the foot o' a sock on the top o' the flask to try an' keep it warm. Y' got a quarter o' an hour for that bit then at lunch time or dinner time as we called it ye stopped at a quarter past eleven that wis t' give the horses about two hours for to feed. The men got their dinner bit they also got in the hay an' stuff to feed the horses at night. They talked about workin' ten hours a day but sometimes it wis far longer than that because you'd an hour in the mornin' before you worked an' then you'd almost another hour at night fillin' up the horse, groomin' them an' that an' it was worse still

if you had a horse standin' in the stable 'cause you had to take it out t' water. Y' see sometimes you were only workin' with one horse and the other one was left in the stable and of course there wis no water in the stable you'd t' take it out to a trough. At one o'clock the foreman would shout 'bridal'. You'd put your watch right by the foreman's watch it didn't matter whether his was the right time or not.

I'm almost certain that I only had one pair o' beets at that time an' I can remember when there wis snow on the ground, 1925 I think, it wis a bad winter an' the farmer kept us in in the mornin' cleanin' cattle courts an' if you've ever seen a cattle court, it's steamin', the dung's as high as those tables there and it's steamin' hot an' you was on that in the mornin' an' then you wis oot in the afternoon t' pick turnips oot the snow. An' I'd reckon they'd be better dein' it the other way roond. I can remember bein' bad wi' chilblains an' they had all sorts o' cures, they (the chilblains) were hellish, y' hands and y' feet were all itchy, itchy and sore and I was told to pit ma feet in the potty or run on the floor! I did baeth o'em but they didna cure ma chilblains!

What we used t' do wis t' put a handful o' hay in t' y' boots, and that was quite a help if yer boots was big enough.

THE rapid march of mechanisation in farming during the war years was strikingly shown at the Lower Deeside champion ploughing match, held at Milltimber Farm on Saturday, when

Anyway, you'd work till five o'clock in the field which could be quite a bit away an' you'd the horses to sort. But when I was at school, we dashed home an' had something to eat and then went back up to the stable. Y' each had a man who y' went wi and y' bedded up the horses ready for them comin' in an' replaced the hay in the hakes an' things like that.

We got a hurl hame on the followin' horses back. That wis your payment for it. We used t' enjoy it an' the men must have enjoyed it too.

Top: Three blacksmiths
Centre: A ploughing match in 1945 at Lower Deeside showing the rapid march of mechanisation.
Bottom: Land army girl, Mrs. Margaret Simpson ploughing in 1943.

David: What about the other jobs you had to do like the maintenance of equipment?

Adam: Well, the ploughs were made o' malleable iron. I jist remember, these Ransom's ploughs were cast so that when the souch wis done or the point wis done y' jist threw it on the scrap heap. In ma father's day they used t' have to take their plough, 'irons' they called them, the culter and the souch t' the blacksmith and that wis done at night after workin' time, y' took it t' the blacksmith and he obviously worked at night and y' told him what you wanted. A lot o' these men were great plough men, they went t' ploughin' matches and things. They went to the blacksmith and as regulars, they could win the ploughin' match, I mean the blacksmith could because they could make your irons spot on an' he'd tell ye t' come back the night before the match an' they would put the finishing touches an' if he didna like y' he'd pit the finishin' touches wrong!

David: What did you have for dinner and what did you have for your tea?

Adam: Well, we usually started with Scotch broth. I don't think that my mother ever bought anything else but boilin' beef. We had sixteen bags o' tatties a year in the Lothians I think both Midlothian and Eastlothian had that. Women had eight bags. And what y' did wis y' used some o' these tatties, what you thought you would use, and sell the rest t' the farmer an' that bought y' your cords for the winter. You wore cord trousers an' you bought them from somewhere in Edinburgh and you got a pair of trousers for about fifteen shillings. When they were worn out y' used them for stackin' an' y' put big patches on your knees for workin roond the stacks. Y' see the whole harvest was stacked at that time outside in the stackyard.

Mrs Nicol: I stayed at home for a while, then people were being called up for war work. Some people if they worked in the food industry, a baker or suchlike, you were exempt. I wanted to do my part you know, but I hated to be away from home, the only thing I could think of which would mean that I could be at home at weekends was the Land Army, which was very much needed. And all the Services, the WRVS, the ATS, all got a gratuity, except the Land Army! My goodness, it was hard work! Most of the girls came from the town like I did. First of all I went onto a farm until there was a vacancy at the College of Agriculture.

Then I went for a month to another farm at Glenkindie on Donside. Then we had to go out to Craibstone, a bit of a waste of time, everyone had to go there whether we were working on a farm or in horticulture just to let them know what was to be expected of them. I did try milkin' a cow, ugh, I didn't like it!

Man: Part o' yir wages wir made up o' feed. Perks, tatties an oatmeal an milk.

David: And how many people would have been in that (the chaulmer)?

Peter Rennie: Well ... just before the start o the War, whin things startit improvin, ye know, the farmers were poor off at the beginnin of the '30s too, an they startit buildin these chaulmers out in the .. well they were usually built at the back o the midden dyke. Ye know whir I am? But ... it was a small building built o stone an lime, an one side of it consistit of a double bed and the other side consistit of a double bed. Ye see whit I mean ... an there was a fireplace at one side an there was a space at the back of the door where eh there was a metal basin where you washed.

Man: A urinal basin... (laughter)

Peter: Well the water hud to come (....) If you were lucky yi see, you kept in with the farm girl, the farm skivvy, an you kept in with her, an ye (....) whiles got washed in the kitchen, see whit I mean? But ye were meant to wash at the back o the chaulmer door ... there was a table at the back o the door ... in 't hud a hole in the centre of it to hold the basin, ye know where I am? An you were supposed t' wash there.

David: Where did you get your hot water from?

Peter: Well. (all laugh) If ye kept in wi' the skivvy yi got it from her, ye see whit I mean? Ye got yer bed an ... yir bed was actually made of .. .caff ... caff, d'ye know what that is? It's the outer covering of the grain. Caff. It came off the threshing mill ye see. An the beds were filled at the end of the year in the month of September, October when the hairst wis in, the caff wis put intae these double beds.

Woman: An you used to sink into them.

David: As you were over the stables there was some heat came up ...

Peter: Yes. But it had its drawbacks too ye see. Because the horse in below ye hid itchy feet ... in the winter time they hid itchy feet ye know whit I mean? The mud collected, in below the hairs in their feet ye see, an ... if this dried it caused an itch ye see. An they used t' knock on the cursy stones with their feet ... an you were disturbed by THEM ye see whit I mean. It had its drawbacks. In if ... you rose it sic an unearthly hour in the morning if ye wasn't really wakened an yi hudn't yir laces tied, yi sometimes fell down the stair an inti the middens.

Man 2: I worked for George Gable an' sons and I was drivin' agricultural stuff, feed stuff out to the farms, feed stuff for cattle, poultry, and sheep an' stuff like that and you'd take back potatoes to Aberdeen city or further south, Glasgow usually, or grain for the oatmeal mills which were at Alford, Palmerston Road, Bridge o'Don, different mills. Different mills accepted different grain. McDonald Alford o' Garioch meal mill would only accept the best o' grain. The Co-operative mill up Palmerston Road would more or less tak anything. The North Eastern Agricultural Co-op would only accept good grain. They weren't oatmeal millers they were agricultural merchants and they dressed grain to resell it back to the farmers as seed oats. The stuff that didn't pass for seed oats was sent either for feedin' stuff for animals or oatmeal for humans.

If it was a slack time in agriculture you went and drove timber out o' the forests to Nigg boxes for the fish trade.

Land girls in Aberdeenshire - 1943

View of Crombie Mills

TEXTILES

At one time the manufacture of textiles was the most important industry in Aberdeen. During the early 19th century approximately 12,000 people were employed in the production of linen, cotton and woollen goods by ten main local manufacturers.

Of these, only two businesses survived the economic depression of the mid-19thcentury; the linen firm of Richard and Company at Broadford and the woollen factory established by John Crombie at Grandholm Mills, Woodside.

The Crombie family developed Grandholm Mills into one of the most modern post First World War factories in the North East of Scotland with a progressive policy of social welfare for employees.

By the 1930's the works at Grandholm had been expanded to cover an area of 400,000 square feet, where high quality flannels and tweeds were produced in one of the few woollen factories to undertake all stages of the processes from raw fleece to woollen cloth.

During the depression the number working at Grandholm fell from over a thousand to between 600 and 800 and short-time working affected most workers.

Bill Morrice recalls what it was like in Aberdeen during the depression for the unemployed and those on short time.

However, things were not all bad and the good intentions of the Crombies were often borne out at this time:-

Bill Morrice: The good thing was that at that time orders were slack and what they did (at Grandholm), they put you on; fortnight on the dole and six weeks working, so they retained the workforce, the second week you were on the brew, they took money out of the Ross Crombie Fund and gave you some to boost your wages.

They were treated terrible ... you went in front o' committees 'n a'thing an' you'd t' prove that you'd looked for work, ken, when there was nae work t' dee. When you were paid they threw the money at yer.

At first you went doon t' the Unemployment Exchange at the bottom o' Market Street but they treated you terrible there. You had t' say "No work", a'body kent there was nae work.

We (at Crombies) were more fortunate because we were Crombies an' got treated a bittie better. We finished up by bein' paid at Crombies, they shifted oot there, an' we signed on at Crombies, y' see this wis the power o' Ross. But the other unemployed were treated terrible.

Grandholm had a long tradition of paternalism similar to that of Bournville. The director of Crombies, J. A. Ross, had always been keen to continue this ethic.
Professor Ian Richardson was in the Department of General Practice at Aberdeen University when he took on the post of honorary medical advisor to the Crombie Mills.

Professor Ian Richardson: When I went to the mill first and met the great John A. Ross, who said to me there was a long tradition of, 'care' was the word he used, for the work people, they had a full time qualified nurse, and were encouraged to go to the medical room as it was called, with any complaint. There were no holds barred, the only thing of course was that I was not to infringe on their own family doctors, which was understandable. I went down every Tuesday morning and the nurse had lined up ten or fifteen people for me to see, people that she felt she wanted to have a doctor's opinion on. Now the first category was minor illness, headaches, indigestion, coughs, colds, so we kept a limited range of medicines to deal with these. Secondly, I saw everybody who had been off work with any serious illness and I introduced a sickness absence record system. Until then it was disorganised and at least now we had complete records of who was off when. For example, one of the foremen, an extremely good craftsman, very important to the mill, who was in charge of the cashmere; he took a massive coronary and was very fearful about returning to work. So I had a long counselling session with him, took his bloodpressure, checked his heart, and then I went to the work's manager and I said, "Look, I think this man can come back to work, and here are the conditions; he'll start work an hour later than anyone else and also he's to be released an hour before." Because as you can imagine seven hundred people coming to work, overloading the transport system and very few of the workers had cars in those days. Well, I like to think that I helped him back to full time work.

Also, there was a very good attitude to employing the disabled at Crombies. I had a great interest in the disabled and I had a special clinic in the hospital for disabled people and we settled them in work.

I came to know the place, it was a good place to work. The workers were carefully recruited, they werent that well paid but there was a real pride in the making of Crombie cloth.

...even though Mr. Ross could be a hard task master there was a benevolence that to me was never in any way suggestive of charity. It wasn't done for productivity, it was done because the management felt a responsibility towards what Mr. Ross used to call "our family".

Valerie Plante: How old were you when you started at Grandholm?

Ellen Grant: Fourteen. I was born in 1927 so I started work in 1941. When I left school I jist walked right into Grandholm.

The supervisor said, "You've got a sister workin' here haven't ya." "Yes" I sez. "Well you'll get a job here then." You'd get a job if you got a sister or a mother there.

Valerie: How long did you train for?

Ellen: You only got three months trainin', that made y' twistin' oot an' in the machine but then it wis big machines efter at, bit I wis nae on em 'cause they wis too heavy for me so I wis pit on the twister an' I wis pit on these cones. There were three strands an y' twist em a' together. They jist showed y' fit t' dee, we'd dee 'at an' they showed y' how t' twirl it on an pit on your string an' let it away good. Y' learnt it in nae time at a'.

Y' got an hours break, the first time it wis only half an hour an then y' a quarter o' an hour for your tea an' y' got a break in the efterneen but y' didna get away from your machine y' jist sat doon aside it an' y' didna get t' smoke bit a cause a lot o' em gid ben an' smoked in the toilets. That's why I hated goin' t' the toilet 'cause the smoke stuck t' your claes. The gaffer would say, "You've been haein a sly smokey." An' I sez, "Nae me, I dae like at fruit." He said "Fit de y' mean?" I said "I'll eat sweets, an' I'll eat apples, crisps but not a smoke." Then he gis doon t' ma sister on her machine an' he sez, "Aye, wi the smell o' it Ellen's been haein a smokey." She sez, "No Alfie, that's one thing we dinna like. Ellen an' me disna like that kinda fruit."

Valerie: It wasn't really so much for your health, it was for your safety?

Ellen: Aye it wis safety fa the mill y' see 'cause it wis aye all ower the fleer. (Wool waste.)

Valerie: They encouraged you to be healthy though didn't they? I read that they gave milk—

Ellen: O aye they gave me milk, I aye got milk. Because I wis weak. I used t' gi doon t' the nurse every day an' I used t' get cream aff a' the milk. When I went t' the canteen I used t' get cream there wi ma dinna she med sure I hid ma dinna an' soup an' puddin'.

Valerie: So the nurse looked after you then.

Ellen: Aye, she wis an auld, auld woman. I used t' g' ben t' get masel weighed. "Oh, you're up in weight, you're up in weight." The nurse would say. I was under weight, I was only aboot six stone something.

Valerie: Did you have to pay for the milk?

Ellen: No, all them that had jist left the school got es bottles o' milk.

Valerie: Did you work there till you got married?

Woman on Twister

Ellen: Aye I got married then I worked back here again. Then I fell wi Albert so I finished work then for a while. I didna hae naebody t' watch my bairn. There wis nae Mither-in-law or naethin' like that 'cause my Mither-in-law died, ma Father-in-law wis blind so there wis naebody t' watch my bairns.

Valerie: When did you go back to work then?

Ellen: When Alec wis sax an' at nights. I gid doon at night, Mary told me, she said, "There's a job on at night" so through the wik there wis a job on at nights spinnin'. So I got this job for three wiks an' Mary she sez t' me, "I've a job in the twister." So I did that but when I gid back the gaffer wisnae affa pleased so he wis standin' behind my back every time I wis workin' sayin' "Y' canna even keep yer ends up, y' canna keep yer ends up." I said, "Would you get aff my back or I wonna work avar?" He said, "Y' surely think you're big?" I said "No, I'm married to a man who telt me that neen o' you should sit on me, so I'm nae gettin' sat on so, either get awar or I'll report you to Tony Weir." So he moved awar.

Valerie: Why was he doing that?

Ellen: He'd jist taen a pick at me. Mary ma sister, she sez, "It's a bloody shame Ellen's gettin' a' the worst work," but she sez, "Dinna worry though Ellen wanna let him aff wi' much she'll let him hae it." So I cerried on workin', it wis a' the worst o' work y' see. So, I kept dein it an dein it an' that's when he turned t' me so efter at I got the best o' work.

Valerie: How many people did you work with?

Ellen: O, there wis aboot twenty, thirty in the shed. It wis really cold 'cause I mean it wis stone floors. It didna matter what y' had on, maybe two or three jumpers an' still you'd be cald. On top o' that I'd an overall an' a bag which kept the ile affa ye'. It wis a dirty job. I'd boots an' thick stockings on ma feet.

Stanley Milton started at Crombie aged 14 in 1939 and was apprenticed as a loom tuner in the weaving department. After becoming a foreman he later became works manager.

Stanley Milton: I knew a bit about weaving, but …. it was really part of the tuning. Being a loom tuner and knowing what happened to the cloth. When I got demobbed, they decided to put me round the mill before I went back to finish my apprenticeship and so I was put into different departments to learn a bit about them. Now, in the finishing department I was put on with this girl who was

Top: Knocking off in the late 1940's.
Bottom: Weaving yarn into cloth.

operating a cutter … she started the cutter but forgot to start the lifter and the cloth got tighter and tighter and I was saying, "What's happening?" I mean, I could see what was happening and it just ripped right across, RRRRRRGH! Well, she broke down in tears! And I stood like a fool, wondering you know, I didn't even know how to stop it and the foreman came in and said, "Now lassie, we all make mistakes!" And after he was away and everything was going, she says, "You might have been upset at me crying" and I said, "I was!" She says, "You see, if I hadn't have cried I'd have got the sack" …. So if she'd stood there and smiled, she may have been dismissed there and then.

Valerie Plante: So, If a man had made the mistake that she made, he'd probably have got the sack would he?

Stanley: Well the assumption was in those days a man wouldn't make that mistake!"

Valerie: Were there women in different jobs to what there had been when you went away during the war, you know, in some departments they hadn't been before?

Stanley: By tradition, there were certain jobs that women did and certain jobs that men did. If there was any heavy lifting to be done it tended to be men (...) yes women came into various other departments, finishing, carding, again the carding condenser rollers got so heavy the women couldn't lift them.

Betty Gordon who started at Grandholm in 1933 when she was fourteen and worked there for five years remembers how she hated working in the department where the fleeces were sorted and blended.

Betty: The wool sortin' shoulda been done by a man, shouldna been for a woman avar 'n I jest didna like it. Fleece wis comin' oot here! Oh my God, it wasna a job for a woman av' all!

Bill Morrice: I started at Grannam (Grandholm) in 1928 (as a wool sorter) and the wages at that time was three pound a week. Well things were a bit tight with the management, they come roond an said, 'Right, we're sorry we've got t' decrease the wages o' five shillin's (25p) Now, five shillin's was a lot at that time so we got in touch wi' Angus McDonald and John McGillivray, who were the great ones in the trade unions organising committee, part o' the Trades Council. And we arranged a meetin' in the Burgh Hall, Woodside, in 1938. Big meetin' it was an they were a' for jinin' the union, ken? There was one o' the lads Dawson

Wool sorting from a container

fae Broadford ... Now the management at Grannam inherited a family outlook like Rowntrees y'ken, wi' holiday pay, we'd sickness benefit and a pension scheme. But the fact that they could say t' ye you're gettin' a decrease in wages wis nae right. An' the manager, the top boy was a lad Meston, an' he got word o' the meetin'. The next mornin' he did his usual stroll roond the works 'believe you had a union meetin', you dinna want a union, jist come t'me'. you know who I am, jist come t'me ' He went roond a'body. By the time he got roond there was only twelve o' us left in the union. It was all young uns ken and somebody telt us about a group o' communists at the Central Study Club and one o' these lads was Johnny Londragan. He went doon there an' said, 'Look', an' he put us in touch with Angus McDonald and John McGillivray. We went to their meetin's an' they said 'Fit we'll dee, we'll visit the factory, we'll meet at the 'Queen' on Sunday mornin' an' we'll get members fae the Biler Makers an' a' the different unions an' we'll visit six people who work in the factory.' We did this for months an' months till finally

in 1938 we got enough in, I think it was a hundred to form a branch and that's how we started. Now the management at Grannam they never said you canna jine a union but they were clever the way they played it, but the ultimate thing was that we finally got an agreement and it became a condition of employment, you'd either got to be a member o' a trade union or there wis some o' the members o' the Plymouth Brethren an' they'd make their union allowance to a charity. So we finally had an agreement that if ony one come doon to work at the mill the personnel officer would hand him a union form and say this is a union place and unless you've got any religious objections you'd to jine the union.

Trevor: Did they take a reduction in wages at the end of the day ?

Bill Morrice: O, we couldna do ony thing aboot it, it was imposed, they said, "I'm sorry about this," but it was imposed.

Gladys Christie: My two sisters, Annie and Ella were there in the weavin' .... your piece had t' be through into the peerk by 12 o'clock. If it wasna through the peerk by twelve o'clock, ye didna get paid. Ye guid without a wage, which was hard, especially far there wis a big family. And mony a time y' see, Annie would come home without her pay. Sometimes they baeth landed without pay. No, my mother had said, she didna want any mair (children) in the weavin'.

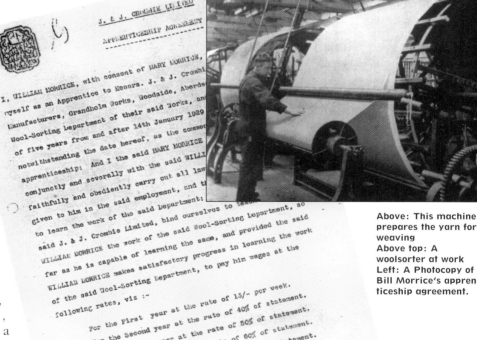

Above: This machine prepares the yarn for weaving
Above top: A woolsorter at work
Left: A Photocopy of Bill Morrice's apprenticeship agreement.

She came doon with me, see, an then I just got into the peerk.

You see, that's what was t' dee wi' Crombies. Lang ago, they got away wi murder - till the union come in. I jined the union because it did us a favour. Mebbe, mebbe it got rough shod later on, I mean, unions are unions, but I mean, it certainly did us a favour for a start.

I was jist an ordinary sewer for a start. O, it took a fair while t' dee a piece, dependin' fit like it was. Some o' them were picky some o' them werna dependin' on the material, dependin' on the thread. But suitings were murder! My fingers have been bleedin' wi suitings, jist wi rubbin'. An irons in your hand, see you jist did it, like 'at ken an you jist rubbed it like that ... feelin' for knots — cause efter it wis clean and a' thing you opened em up sewed in the bitties and cut em off.

Richards & Co at Broadford works developed into one of the largest linen manufacturers in Scotland, surviving with difficulty the economic climate at the end of the 19th century by specialising in the production of raw flax to the finished article, of coarse linen fabric, sail cloth and canvas hose.

By the 1950's, although the workforce had been reduced from over 2,000 to around 1,000, Richards and Co. at Broadford still had the largest industrial labour force in Aberdeen.

Lizzie Findlayson: No smoking was allowed in the factory, owing to the nature of our materials. It was the practice of smokers to slip into the toilets for a quick puff. One day three of us were having a quick draw, when the gaffer came into the ladies room, shouting and swearing, "I know you're smoking," he yelled and even tried to push open the bolted cubicle doors. We had to come out, minus, of course, the cigarette. We knew the penalty for smoking was instant dismissal, but Jimmy couldn't prove it. He ordered us back to our looms, but that was not the end of it.

Next morning, Jimmy got revenge! As we went to our stations at 7.45, he came across to our squad, and pointing a finger at each of us, said "follow me", and led us to the dreaded tower. We had to climb at least one hundred steps to get there, and it was absolutely the worst place I had ever worked in. Flapping belts drove the machines and we had to activate them manually. We were each sent to a different corner of the huge room, and only had time for a quick word in the ten minute tea break. We had to ascend or descend these hundred steps four times daily. Although there was a lift for material being

Top: Advert. Canvas for all purposes.
Middle: 'Brushing up' - the last process before the cloth goes into the warehouse
Bottom: Cloth in the warehouse, ready for dispatch

transferred up or downstairs, the personnel were not allowed to use it, as it was deemed to be too dangerous. A young lad had been killed while using it illegally a few months earlier. We had been in this hell-hole for a few weeks when the gaffer Jimmy came up, and told us we could go to our former machines downstairs. What a relief that was. We didn't go for a smoke, three at a time after that!

I was on my own, at forty, with three boys to bring up, so I needed more money to keep things going, than I could earn working at home. I was given a place in a day nursery for the youngest boy, at six months of age. The hours were 8am to 5pm. The other two boys were at school.

I was sent by the employment exchange to the Broadford mills, in Maberly Street. Those were textile weaving mills. I was put on a trance machine which made ribbons of flax-like appearance, from waste material. The ribbons passed from my machine to the roving one, where they were twisted into a thin cotton cord and spun on to bobbins. There were, I think about fifty huge bobbins for empty ones. They were called shifters. The full bobbins went to another department to be spun, from the spinners on to the weavings. From the office one could order materials for dressmaking or even towels or blankets.

Another department made hosepipes, which I was told was a very hard job. There were many accidents mostly minor, although I did see a married woman who came from Stonehaven, lose her left hand, apart, that is, from her thumb. All the way to hospital she kept asking about her wedding ring, they found it amongst the waste material, that she had been putting through the carding machine. She had been sweeping the machine while it was on, thus breaking the safety rules.

Woman: I startit at Broadford when I was fourteen an' I got ten shillin's a week an' I used t' rush home on a Thursday with my pay, I was the oldest in a family of five and we didn't have a lot of money at that time so my mother was very glad when I startit workin' I tell y'. I got a shillin' pocket money an' my mither had nine shillin's. I was born 1912 so I startit work in 1926.

Above: Newspaper cuttings showing life in the Flax Mill.

Trevor: So what did you do at Broadford ?

Woman: I was a reeler, then I went on t' piece-work as a reeler. I never used t' look up from ma work 'cause I was wantin' t' mak a lot o' money, so I never stayed off ma work or onything like that.

Before you could be a reeler, y' had t' go on t' tiein' knots. That was ma first job, tiein' special knots afore I could go on t' the reelin'. I startit at eight o'clock in the morning pit on your apron and you'd t' work till quarter past twelve and take till quarter past one for lunch. I used t' walk all the way there an' back to work from Wales Street to Maberly Street in hail, rain or shine.

When I was about eighteen I went intae makin' gloves at the glove factory in Rose Street. It wis piece work there as well. I made the fingers in the fingerin' department. I made the fingers about half way up in the long glove, remember the long glove? I worked there till I got married when I was twenty six.

Margaret Mutch: I worked in a shop before the war then I had t' go into the services or into war work. Ma father didna approve goin' into the services so he got me a job in Broadford's on the reeler and worked for quite a while then I wis shifted down to the twister. The material cam in an' come doon into a bobbin an' twists a' the stuff t'gither. Then I had an accident an' I lost a finger so I wasna workin' for a while then when I went back t' work but I wouldna g' back t' the machines so I was paintin' bobbins. The work at Broadfords was war work 'cause they made hose pipes and the khaki for the uniforms.

David: What materials did they use for that?

Margaret: It wasna material when I started, it was jist the flax an that gon' intae yarn for makin' things y'see.

But they had all the orders for that kinda things.

Professor Ian Richardson: (Whilst in the position of medical adviser to J & J Crombie) I was asked to advise a very old established firm in Aberdeen with an unfortunate reputation; Richards Limited. The working conditions were some of the poorest in Aberdeen. You only went there if you couldn't get anything else. I went along and was shocked, it was like something out of the dark ages, the early industrial revolution. The flax was brought in and the first thing that happens to the flax is that it gets the daylight beaten out of it by machinery which takes off the hard outer cover and inside is the fibre that goes to make the canvas. You could hardly see, it was like going into a dense fog! And I made some enquiries about byssinosis, this disease of the lungs is due to flax dust, and there were three or four cases of it. So to cut a long story short, that was put right, exhaust ventilation was put in and that dealt with that side of things.

There were other parts of that factory with which I was unhappy. There was a lot of unguarded machinery, well, again that was dealt with. And then I said, "I think you should have a full-time nurse and you should have a medical department 'cause there is a lot of minor injuries here and they are not being treated." Well there was a disused building right in the centre of the works and they converted it and made a beautiful medical department, first class! In fact the Lord Provost of Aberdeen came and opened it.

I like to think that my experience at Crombies helped to make Richards the modern human place to work it is now.

Work in general

Other industries

John Londragan: I first started work, it's incredible, when I look back on it, fin I first started work as a young lad amidst the mules at the bakery, the bakery amidst the mules there, I got seven and six a week. Now think of it, seven and sixpence a week. Fit would that be now? (37.5p) Of course the difficulty makin' (...) because of the values you could buy more at that time even for seven and six than you could at the present time ...

Now for that seven and six I started work at six o' clock in the mornin', this is when I started, six o'clock in the morning and I didn't finish until half past twelve or quarter to one the following mornin'. That's right because we went out the country we used to go to Culter and Skene with the two horses an the van an that ye know ... the van boy an that there ... this was Monday, Tuesday, Thursday, Friday and Saturday. An Widnesday, it was ma half day. An Widnesday it was startit at the same time but it finished at half past six at nicht, at was ma half day! An the Sunday I hid to go up to the Denburn ... where the horses were stabled... and my job was to clean the van oot and clean the horses doon an everything on a Sunday morning this is fae aboot nine o'clock 'till aboot the back o' twelve for seven an six a week. That's what I was bein' paid.

Top: What was on in the early '50's!
Bottom: A dance at the Music Hall, Aberdeen

Nancy: I met my husband at work, so he used t' meet me and take me home. This was at Cordiners. It was a big romance and I was married by the time I was nineteen.

Vera Hunter: There wis nae hanky panky that days!

Trevor: You can't have all met your men at work, where did you meet anyone?

Woman: The dancing.

Woman: Yes the dancing.

Vera Hunter: Did y' nae walk the mat?

Women: Aye, yes we did.

Woman: Yes every Sund'y, y' jist wasted y' shoe leather.

Woman: Y' met y' friends—

Vera: Y' musta got a lad at sometime—

Woman: Y' did but it wasna serious.

Woman: I worked in the canning factory, Marshall's canning factory.

Woman: Did you work there as well?

Woman: It was the time the war was on. The small herrin'.

Woman: The spratties, aye, we did that when the war was on for the rations for the soldiers and I was on the machine. The girls packed the beef an' carrots an' every thin' inta the tin an' then it cam right roond t' me, an' it wis all cooked in this machine at the end. Then the girls took them off and packed them inta boxes. They were then sent away t' sodgers and the girls used t' write their names on the label for any soldier y' know that would get them.

Trevor: Did anyone get an answer?

Eva Mclean: Yes I think so but I can't remember right now. Then the time came that they were takin' the girls on to the buses so it wis jist aboot a month before that, that the boss of the canning factory, Robertson, he cam in aboot an' said that we were over the target that week. So he pit a little extra in oor pay packets.

But I had ma mind made up t' go onta the buses. So I went doon t' get an interview an' I got the job. When I went back to tell them, Robertson said, "Don't y' think you've left us a bit dirty?" An' I sez "No, I'm only tryin' t'

Photograph of Eva Mclean in clippie's uniform.

better ma self, I won't better ma self here!" (laughter) So I'm on the buses now (1941?) so Mr. Robertson and Mr. Bruce, they cam on the bus an' Robertson sez t' Bruce, "D' y' recognise her?" And of course he looked and said, "That wis yer operator on the machine an' he sez, "Wid y' like t' come back." An' I sez, "No thank you!" (laughter) I enjoyed the buses, aye, I stayed for five years.

Trevor: Why did y' come off the buses?

Eva: The men come back, so when the men come back the women had t' move over. The men were jist aboot back (from the war) an' there wis aboot twelve o' us left so I got word there was a chap who opened up a restaurant jist on the Esplanade there. He knew ma father an' he said, "Y' daughter will be leavin' the buses shortly d'y' think she'd come an' work with us. So, I hadna done restaurant work so I thought I'll give it a try so I give it a try. It was called Mac McWilliam on the Esplanade.

Eva: On the Esplanade there they used t' mak a huge pot o' soup in Mac's restaurant an' we used t' queue t' get a bowl o' soup.

Woman: Well, there was the hotdogs, the men frae Lewis' an' a' them cam t' get them.

Trevor: So all the women who were employed in men's jobs had to give them up at the end of the war and let the men continue their jobs?

Eva: Oh yes.

Trevor: Did y' think that was fair?

Above: At work in the co-op dairy
Above left: 'Our Service to You as Dairymen.' Part of an advert for the Baritone Co-op.

Eva: Oh yes, we were jist keepin' their jobs.

Woman: After I was married, I had a spell o' workin' in the Co-op milk and I loved it. The only thing I didna like when I first went there was the horses. I wis terrified o' them but then when they went onto the electric buggies, it wis brilliant. I've seen us goin' up to the knees in snow, an' I mean snow. It wis commin' up ta Christmas time, the other three girls that wis there, their family an' my two boys used t' come an' help 'cause you couldn't get through the snow. You only got one day off an' that was New Year's day y' worked on Christmas day y' see. It was a hard job but it was a super job because you met so many people.

General Factory Work

Lizzie Findlayson: I left school at the age of 14. Being the eldest of five, I had no chance of staying on for further education, as I would have liked. There were vacancies at the local box making factories, but I thought I'd get something better. I heard of an office girl vacancy in a publishing firm and applied and was accepted. After all I had a merit certificate, which was something great in these days. I rushed home to tell my mother, but when I told her the wages were six shillings (30p) weekly, she nearly hit the roof. Fiddes Sawmill were paying 10 shillings (50p) and I was told I'd have to go there. Although I protested it was of no avail. I trudged back to town and had to refuse the offer.

I duly started in Fiddes Sawmill, as a catcher at a crosscut saw, then catcher at a rotary printing machine before getting a press machine of my own. My wages were now 18 (90p) shillings. The noise in the factory was excessive. The screeching of the saws, thumping and clicking of the printers, the double wail (hee haw) of the dove tailers and worst of all the pneumatic air pistols rat-a-tat on the bottle boxes, which had wire divisions.

The electricity for the factory was produced by steam from Fiddes' own boiler house. If for any reason the steam went down, the lights would flicker and go out and the machines would grind to a halt. The mill was cold and draughty. The dim lights were kept on all day. Upstairs was the box making, which were all piecework. I asked to be transferred, as I was sure I could earn more, but was refused with many excuses. I decided to look for another job.

Isobel Sim: Well I worked in Paterson's Sawmill, y' know where the Gateway is now in Wellington Road, that was a sawmill, Paterson's. I actually dressed boards. Y' know the boards that's in between the bales of cloth. We had t' get the sawers to cut the length of boards. Then we had t' carry a bundle up t' the loft then we'd to cut weer own paper an' that was on a big table an' it wis measured out in inches. There was a big blade we called the guillotine. I sliced ma finger on it, I was fooling around I wasna lookin' I reached for the handle t' cut the paper an' er sliced m' finger so I was rushed t' the hospital t' get it stitched up. So, we had t' put the paper on the table. We'd a bowl o' batter wi a brush in the batter. You'd put the board on the table put the batter all round, dress the board an' take it up. I think we got about twopence. (Less than 1p.)

Isobel Sim and friends on a cart in the wood yard

Trevor: Each one?

Isobel: Oh, no, no, no, no, for about a dozen I think. In between that we did time work. We got twopence an hour. Y' had t' be there a year and wait till the manager was in a good mood before you asked the manager for another ha'penny an hour to make it up to twopence halfpenny an hour. We had t' carry battens on wir shoulders from the yard t' the men who was workin' the saws. It wis heavy work wasn't it but we'd a good time, we used t' sing an we were all friends.

Trevor: Was this work that men normally did?

Isobel: No, this was 1936 when I wis fourteen. That's the kinda work we had t' do. Piece work, an' we were lucky if we made 50 pence, ten shillin's y'know.

Trevor: How many people did you work with?

Isobel: Well, maybe that wis aboot twenty girls y'know. We were all in a loft an' we'd one manager over us. The men worked the saws down stairs an' they cut the wood an' there was lorries. In between that, we used t' point sticks an' Nancy said they got sixpence (2.5p). We got fourpence (1.6p) for a crate an' that wis forty eight bunches o' sticks. Y' took your sticks an' y' put them in this machines wi a pedal an' pit a wire round it an' tied it up.

We used t' cheat, we used t' have oor crates the one side an the gaffer would come an' check em. We'd wait till he went away then we'd take crates from over here an' put them over there! (Laughter) Jist t' make that extra shillin'. We had t' do it t' get a wage.

Vera Hunter: Survival, was it?

Isobel: Survival, aye.

Woman: Are you glad that somebody else cheated an' maybe sneak a few sticks fa y' mither?

Vera: Did y' nae get a bunch o sticks hame?

Woman: No.

Woman: Y' didna get a fry o' fish either—

Vera: I bet you cheated an' a'.

Woman: I did, fen I passed ma spinnin' test I pit a fish up ma jumper t' let ma mither ken I could dee it an' it fell oot as I wis commin' oot the door. It wis a whole fish y' see an' I pit it up ma jumper an he sez, (the manager) "Fits this?" Then he sez, "Jist tak it but that's the finish an' dinna tak nae mair." Y' still had ways o' gettin' oot fish.

Woman: When y' were teckin' back y' net (made previously at home) y' felt guilty.

Jesse Watt: When we went oot t' work on a Seterday mornin' we'd do each others hair while y' was doin' somebody

Delivery boys were popular up until the mid 1960s

else's an' oor gaffer one day he sez "Well I don't know what happens in there on a Saturday, they go in with straight hair an' they go oot curly." Someone did your net an' you did someone's hair.

Florence Cumming: I mind fen King George wis dyin' an' we knew it wis announced he wis on his death bed. There wis a shop in Victoria Road that rented oot wireless' bit nae these fancy things we have t'day an' we went t' the boss t' see if we could get one o' these wireless' so we could listen to see fit wis goin' on. An' we were allowed t' use it, we used t' get another station for a bit o' music an' then we'd pit it back an' then when he died a' that y' heard wis Big Ben chimin' an' the tickin' o' the clock an' we were braidin' weer nets t' the tick o' the clock, it wis, "Tick, tock, tick, tock has he died yet?" Gutherie, that's the name o' the shop. I could aye mindin' that then we thought they didn't come for it for a while an' the music wis back on an' we wis braidin' weer nets an' y' know this, he was a very religious man an' teen the wireless awar fae us.

Trevor: Why did he take it away?

Florence: Well, that wis his way, folk jist didna get music at work like they do t'day.

Josephine Robertson: When I left the school I went into A. B. Hutchison's the baker an' went wi rowies et six o'clock in the mornin' wi a basket a' doon Crown Street t' Devanha Gardens deliverin' orders. Then y'd t' come back an' scrub the shop efter at. Well, I wis there aboot a year an' a half. Efter scrubbin' oot the shop they made up the bread for the guest houses in Crown Street an y'd delivered a' at dinner time in a big basket. An' then I went to Mollison's the baker in East North Street jist across fae the auld lodgin' hoose.

They made puddin's an y' had t' weigh them oot a' ready for packin'. After at I went t' the lemonade. I was twenty year in the lemonade. That wis really, really hard work. Sangs, in Seaforth Road that's who I worked for. I labelt the bottles y'ken, they came oota the machines an' came along, look at a' my fingers wi liftin' bottles four a' a time, liftin' em up t' see there wis nae dirt in y' bottle. Y'd t' be very, very quick t' keep up wi the machine. Then y'd t'pack y' cases. There wis twelve in each case, 'cause I wis ae a strong kind o', that's why I'm big noo ken, and y' stacked em. I could jist stack em five high y'd get a boy t' stack em higher an' I wis there twenty years.

Man: As a welder I used to do a lot of work on the steam engines. I worked with the North-eastern Welding Company, I used to work all over, mostly boiler work on the steam engines. Sometimes the engines would get a fracture on the outside edge, and we used to cut it out and fill it up with weldin'. The lorries were steam driven as well as the traction engines. Most people who had accidents mostly got caught in the chains, there were never any guards on them. I remember one fella, he was driving a coal lorry, steam driven, down a steep brae at Stonehaven and the chains broke, and he had no brakes, no way o' stoppin' the thing and he jist had to drive the thing down to the bottom and turn it up on the bank to get it stopped.

Women working at the bottling premises of Messers James Calder & Co., Brewers Ltd. 1943.

Shopwork

Isobel Wallace: I was born and brought up in Aviemore in Invernesshire and I went to school in Rothiemurchus. I left school when I was fourteen and I started in the Co-operative store in Aviemore and I was there for about six years. That was at the war time with all the rationing, the ration books and the points and all this and we used t' spend ages counting all the points. It was a general shop there was drapery there was everything in it. You took turns with everything. It was just girls in the shop and we used t' skin all these cheeses y'know, they were like barrels and we had t' bone all the hams and we were trained really, jist grocers, baggin' all the sugar makin' everything up. It wis very interestin' 'cause y' knew every one in the village. Then my sister left Aviemore and then phoned me t' come through (to Aberdeen). I worked in a house as a domestic for a while and then I finally got a job in Collies in Union Street and I worked at the coffee counter there. It was jist serving teas and coffees. It was a high class shop. Andrew Collie, it's where the book shop is now called Dillons. So I was there till I got married and then I jist left and had ma family.

Agnes Wallace: I left school at fourteen as well and I went for an interview at a ladies dress shop it was known as a gown shop in those days. It was in George Street and I think that my wages were six and sixpence (32.5p) a week. I was there for about three weeks and they must have seen that I was quite a capable person so it was increased to seven and sixpence (35p). An awful lot happened between the ages of fourteen and sixty five but I worked at the same shop for fifty two years.

Trevor: Really, and what was the name of the shop?

Agnes: Mascot fashions. In between, I went to the war early in 1944 until late 1947.

Trevor: What did you do?

Agnes: I was a wireless operator. I was in Bedfordshire and it so happened that I was in the same camp for all the time I was there 'cause it was a specialised job. I was in what was called the 'Y' service and it was a sort of a secret thing but now the war has been over for fifty years we can now discuss it. Then when the war was over I came back to the same place and became the manageress and later, a director of the firm. It was then taken over by somebody else and I then became the supervisor. The man who bought it over had a few shops in various places - it was a very interesting job, I really liked it. I enjoyed my work but I would have liked to have stayed on at school but I had four brothers who were getting a trade so therefore they'd very little wages and it was the norm in those days that a girl didn't really need an education because she'd get married but this (herself) is one lady who didn't get married so it didn't work out. But I did go to evening classes for shorthand and typing and things like that.

Trevor: What was a typical day then, when you worked in a shop?

Agnes: Oh, well, I'd go into the shop at nine o'clock, and I might have cleaned windows, at fourteen. I might have swept and polished the floor. Y'had t' do all these jobs and then we had to deliver goods to customers. You had to be prepared to do anything and everything. In fact one night I had to go t' the country because this lady had t' have this garment on the Saturday night an' I was out in the middle o' the country at eight o'clock at night and I was only fourteen or fifteen.

David: What was your experience of working in a shop?

Betty Allen: Well when you first started you were jist a general little dogsbody. You'd t' sweep the floors an' dust everything that wis on show. When you'd done that y' were put through the back to weigh oot sugar an' peas an' barley an' lentils an' whatnot all into brown bags an' I never mastered the art o' foldin' the bags. You'd be absolutely amazed 'cause I watched an' there was nothing to it. I even had a bag at home wi sand in it an' I still couldna do it! It wis jist a knack, it wis marvellous t' see them pick up a scoop a' stuff an' pit it into a bag an' it wis jist the tiniest bit out. They jist seemed t' know what made a pound or a quarter. It wis the same when they cut up the butter or cheese they'd jist know the right amount, but this bags, they jist had me fair flummoxed!

It wis drummed inta y' that the customer was always right. It didna matter what they said you'd t' agree with them, which I do t' this day. One person cam in an' said "Oh, Bet. it's freezin' oot there." An' I sez, "I know." Somebody else cam in an' said, "What a lovely day." An' I said "Isn't it beautiful." (laughter) Well that's what y' caed diplomacy.

Y' had t' learn t' count accurately. When y' first startit they'd have let y' - someone would have come in for say six or eight items, they woulda let you write it doon on a bit o' paper an count it up but then your boss always checked it an' if there wis as much as one brass ha'penny woe an' betide. If somebody cam in for their weeks shoppin' they were askin' you for somethin' an' you'd be countin' it up in your head as you went along. Y' never had t' stop at the end and count it up. The young kids couldna d' that nowadays, no way.

Joyce Everill: The search for employment among school-leavers today is nothing new. Back in the 1930's it was just as bad. I was lucky, mother came home from paying her papers at the newsagents shop just down Victoria Road where we lived and announced she had a job for me. The assistant was leaving to get married as was the want in those days, and the owner of the shop Mr Leiper, knowing I was leaving school at the end of term had asked her if I would be interested in the job. Would I? You bet I would. Not only was it a job, but my nose was always stuck in a newspaper, magazine or book and I was a regular visitor to the public library as well. I was delighted. I couldn't wait to bid farewell to Torry Intermediate school as it was 1935, and a week after my fourteenth birthday I started work as a shop girl. Monday to Saturday, half days on Wednesdays when most of the shops used to close in the town. The hours were long as the shop had to be opened early in the morning for the passing trade of those going to work, and I wasn't finished until late on a Saturday as we had to wait for the Green Final coming in with all the sports results. It was well after seven before I could count myself free for the week-end. One weeks' holiday in the year during the summer and only New Years day off as a public holiday. Christmas wasn't kept so much then, it was the New Year when everything closed down for the day.

My first job when I arrived at the shop was to clean out the grate and light the wee fire at the back of the counter after fetching coal from the cellar. Then there were the deliveries to be sorted out for the paper-boy to take round the customers who liked their newspapers delivered to the door. Tidy the counter, sweep the floor, dust the shelves, wash the doorstep and clean the big window once or twice a week in between serving customers. All this for the princely sum of six shillings (30p) a week!

A friend went to work in a net making factory when she left school some months after me, and she was paid a much higher wage. But she was paid 'piece work' as it was called. In other words, the harder she worked and the more she produced the more she was paid. But it was hard graft in these net making factories and hard on the lassies hands as well, but at least they didn't have as early a start as I did. I did envy her having a half day on Saturday though. I could only wander up Union Street looking into the windows of the closed shops on a Wednesday. Not that I could have afforded to buy anything, but there was no harm in wishing, was there? What I did enjoy about my job in the newsagents was meeting the different customers every day. There were the regulars who called in every morning for their paper and cigarettes. Players or Capstan for the working man, Passing Cloud for the ladies, Bogey Roll to be cut up and weighed for the fishermen to put in their pipes, and a tuppeny paper packet of Woodbine for the young lads. Cigars and Cheroots for the businessmen - and my granda who always called in past on his way up to the top storey to our flat.

Fishermen, home to land their catches would tell me, "Saw your dad up in

Lerwick", or wherever they had happened to be, and I would carry the news home to mum.

I worked in that shop for two years until the bosses daughter left school and I was handed my cards along with my wages and told I was no longer required as she would be working there from now on. I didn't know whether to be sad or glad for jobs were still scarce then, but there was a world out there waiting to be explored, and I was eager to find out what lay across the Dee then. Small though my wages were, it was better than being on the dole which was even less, so it wasn't a very rosy outlook for me. Worse was having to go home and tell mum I'd got the sack, but she just gave me a look and said, I thocht this wid happen fin his ain lassie left the school. Niver mind, something else'll turn up.

It did, in the guise of the traveller from John Menzies the wholesale newsagents and booksellers in Stirling Street. On learning I had no job he sought me out and offered to put in a good word for me with the Manager who was taking on extra staff for the Christmas and New Year period. I went for an interview and was taken on for four weeks at ten shillings a week. Suddenly everything looked brighter even if it was only temporary, and what was more, we had Saturdays for a half-day! I would have gladly stayed on permanently, and in fact Mr Harley kept me longer than the original time set hoping I could be taken on the staff, but the Head Office in Edinburgh decreed otherwise and sadly I had to leave and sign the dole once more. But I had his promise that if he heard of anything in our line he would keep me in mind.

Once again I was back on the dole queue, and with more youngsters having left school that Christmas jobs were still at a premium.

Back in the '30's, if you were unemployed for a few weeks you had to attend what we called the 'Buroo School' in Charlotte Street, and we were given lectures on various subjects. It shows how interesting it was when I can only recall being taught how to bath a baby using a celluloid doll as a model!

It certainly didn't advance my education any, that's for sure, and I have the feeling it was only meant to keep us out of mischief and give us somewhere to go every day more than anything else. Certainly didn't do me any harm though I will admit, and as long as you attended there was no fear of your dole money being cut.

A few weeks there, and I was sent for an interview with Miss Birnie who owned a hat and dress shop in George Street. I was accepted and thus began my brief sojourn into the world of fashion.

I was put on the hat department and quite enjoyed it. It certainly wasn't as hard work as the newsagents, and was shorter hours too. But I was back to Wednesdays for my half-day.

The other girls and I had quite a bit of fun - if we could escape Miss Birnie's eagle eye, she liked her staff to be on their toes all the time even if their were no customers to be served, and I must have rearranged these blasted hats a dozen times a day trying to make myself look busy. Is it any wonder I have never worn a hat since except to a wedding or during my Army days - which is another story!

The wages were seven and sixpence a week, but we could earn a few coppers extra if there was a line that wasn't selling well and we could palm one on to some poor unsuspecting soul. Fridays were the best days for that, as the country lassies came into town hellbent on buying a new hat for the Kirk on Sunday. My but they were a gullible lot, and the guid Lord'll probably niver forgive me for the lies I told them about some of these monstrosities. All for the sake of a few extra coppers on my wages at the end of the week! It's a wonder the milk didn't curdle in the cows udders at the sight of them when they wore them back home!

Of course, there were plenty town lassies who were just as easy led by telling them that such and such flattery and I'd made a sale. The only people I couldn't fool was my own mum and auntie Lizzie when they came in to buy a new hat. They arrived knowing exactly what they wanted and what they could afford, and it was more than my life was worth to try and sell them anything!

My feelings towards the country lassies were radically changed one day though when we went through to the small staff room for our tea and found a big rat sitting calmly in the sink! There was a hasty exit by us screaming females, and a sonsy country lass put down the hat she was trying on and asked what was the matter. We quakingly told her about our unwelcome visitor and she gave a laugh. 'Is that a'?' she asked. 'Far aboot is't' and with shaking hands we pointed to the door. 'Seen sort him oot' she said as she disappeared inside. There was a few bangs and then she reappeared holding one very dead rat by the tail.

'Fit'll I dee wi't?' she asked with a grin, and was directed towards the rubbish bin. She had picked it up by the tail and dashed its brains out on the sink! That was one country lass who went up in my estimation and wasn't palmed off with an unsaleable hat that day. It changed my views on the folks who came in from the country for I would never have had courage to do what she did.

I worked there quite happily for a few months until the Manager of Menzies kept his word and sent for me to tell me there was a vacancy in MacKeggies Bookshop up at Holburn Junction. He told Mr Smart, the owner, about me and gave me a good recommendation. Hopefully I set off to meet him and was offered the job immediately. I was back in my element away from Miss Birnie's hats and rats, and what's more, my wages would be twelve and sixpence a week. A fortune! I handed in my notice to Miss Birnie and went back to my first love, books and newspapers.

The hours were much longer than I had served in the hat shop of course as I had to travel across Market Street and up the length of Union Street to be at the shop for 8am and there was no public transport available as early as that. But rain or shine, I hiked it, rain or shine, using the bus or tram to get home for my lunch and back again. I quickly got to know many of the folks who travelled the same route early in the morning, those employed in the fish trade etc. and was always sure of a cheery 'Aye, aye quine, fit like this mornin?'.

It was a very different clientele I served in that shop. No housewives in their aprons popping for their Peoples Friend or Weekly News, no fishermen for their Bogey Roll to give me news of my dads boat, but folks from the West End of the town. Business men and women, or the gentry from their big houses mainly. But one thing remained the same, if one of the paper-boys didn't turn up I had to sling the heavy bag over my shoulder and get on with the deliveries myself or else the phone would never stop ringing. Woe betide us if a client didn't have his Financial Times to pore over at the breakfast table!

Those trips opened my eyes as to how the other half of the town lived. If the paper was to be put through the front door letter box I would have a quick peep into the huge windows as I passed. My goodness! Such luxury, it took my breath away, and I would regale mum with descriptions of what I had seen. "Aye, it's an ill divided world", she would say, and shake her head.

Some customers demanded that the papers be delivered to the kitchen door, and many a hot cup of cocoa I got from some kind hearted cook on a winter morning. I thought one of the maids was pulling my leg when she told me she had to iron the newspapers each morning before they were laid before the lord and master - but she wasn't!

It was a much bigger shop than the one in Torry and took a lot more hard work to keep things tidy and clean, but I didn't mind. Gladys, the other assistant and I shared the work between us. My one big problem when I first started was the big till with its press buttons and drawer which sprung open when you touched it. Many's a bang in the ribs I got until I mastered the art of standing well away from it! It was no use trying to manicure your nails either, it did it for you! Trimmed them down to the quick if you weren't careful.

It was a cold shop as well with the door always opening, and many's a time I suffered from a bad cold. Mr Smart would send out to the neighbouring chemist for a bottle of cough mixture and would make sure I took it. He was a kind man who looked after his staff well.

My wages were raised to fifteen shillings a week after six months and that made up for the long trek to Torry each morning in my opinion. I'd never had so much money in my life, but mum made sure a little of it was tucked away in the Savings Bank she had started me in whilst at the school. The Penny Bank it was called, and a penny it was which she gave me every Friday to be collected by the teacher, and I've often wondered how many people of my generation started their savings the same way. It was something I was eternally grateful to her for when I got married and came to provide a home for my little family.

Life was good, I was happy in my work, and the newspaper headlines made little impact on a teenager then. Poland? That was the other side of the world as far as I was concerned. Hitler? A funny little man who strutted about like a peacock by what I saw on the newsreels when I was at the cinema. A bit like Charlie Chaplin to me.

I did notice Mr Smart having long serious conversations with some of the customers, and they would shake their heads gravely. He had been an officer during the first World War and no doubt could see what was coming like a lot more of the older generation. There was talk of gas masks and air raid shelters, blackouts etc. but it meant little to me. It wasn't until the 3rd of September 1939 that I discovered what it was all about when I stood with mum and dad beside our wireless and listened to Mr Chamberlain make the announcement that our country was now at war with Germany, and watched the tears run down mum's face.

The next day we couldn't get enough newspapers to satisfy the customers. Every issue was bought up as quickly as we put it in the counter, and all the veterans of the previous war relived their experiences to me over the counter.

The blackout during those Winter months meant that I had to walk over Market Street in complete darkness, but we closed a bit earlier at night, and shopgirls hours were cut to forty eight hours per week. Mr Smart joined the Observer Corps which kept watch for approaching enemy aircraft, and when he was on duty I was entrusted with the days takings until the next day. There was no such things as hole in the wall banking in those days. Mums little suitcase in which she kept birth certificates and bank books etc., now was a safety deposit for the shops money, and I had to carry it back over again next morning. It never gave me a thought, for it was very seldom you heard of such things as muggings in those days. Now I grip my bag with my few shillings in it very tightly indeed for there's never a day but you hear of someone being robbed even in broad daylight.

I was awarded another pay rise to compensate for my extra responsibilities and now took home a whole pound. Pocket money rose accordingly, and out of five shillings a week I bought stockings, paid bus fares, went to the pictures or ice skating and all the little incidents a girl needed back then.

Customers changed too. Many of the big houses in the West End were taken over by the Government to be used as offices or some other facility. In fact, the West End has never been the same since.

Office work

Mary Simpson: I was born in 1930 outside Kemnay but moved into Aberdeen when I was a young girl and lived in a tenement in Rosemount Place. I went to Mile End school till I was thirteen then after that I went to the Central school which used to be in Belmont Street. I took a secretarial course at school, getting shorthand and typing. I left school when I was seventeen in 1947. My friend and I got two interviews, one at the corner of Union Terrace at the insurance company, and we had one at Woolworth's Union Street. So, we went up to the insurance place and had our interviews and they were quite pleased but when we were coming out we were saying, Oh God it was all old men with black suits and everybody was sitting with long faces. "Do you want to work here?" "No I don't want to work here do you?" So we went to Woolworth's 'cause they wanted two people there. We had our interview and we said yes we'll start on Monday. I went home and told my mother and she was not pleased. She said, "I gave you all this education and you go to a place like Woolworth's." And I was in Woolworth's for thirty two years!

Kerstin: Why did she disapprove of Woolworth's?

Mary: Well the shops in Aberdeen y' know, - well I didn't want t' be a shop assistant and the only choices were to work in a factory, shop work or work in offices and once you got a job you stuck at it because if you didn't have a job it could be very difficult just like what it is now. I got married in 1955 then I had to leave Woolworth's because they didn't keep married women on in those days. Eventually I went back when they started takin' back married women.

Kerstin: Could you tell me about your early days in Woolworth's?

Mary: Well, in that days we worked a 48 hour week starting at half past eight in the morning till six

Office workers at the North of Scotland bank in 1945.

o'clock at night. You got time for lunch but there was no canteens or nothin', in that days I went home for lunch. You also got a break, ten minutes in the morning and ten minutes in the afternoon. We also worked a full day on Saturday. We only had Sundays off. When I first started I got seventeen and sixpence a week and when it was my birthday I got it up to a pound. Then when I was made assistant cashier I got another five shillings more.

Kerstin: What could you buy for a pound?

Mary: Well we had to live on a pound, I gave my mother ten shillings which was half for food an' that and she let us keep the other ten shillings which you had t' save for clothes. In the war, when I first started, working clothes were rationed anyway. We had t' make do if you know what I mean. There was very little in the shops, there was no sweets there was no biscuits there wasn't much at all.

Where McDonald's is now, that was Woolworth's, the whole big buildin'. The office, there was six of us in a small space. There was hardly room to move and you stood most of the day there was no room for seats. We went round and collected the cash. In that days there were lots of cash registers all the old fashioned wooden ones. When they went wrong y' took a hammer and hit the thing and it usually worked y' know!

Kerstin: What was the best job working in the office or as a shop assistant?

Mary: In the office. If someone was leaving the office to get married or something maybe six or so people from the shop used t' say, "Can I leave my name or maybe take me into the office?" It wasn't much better paid but it was considered a better job than a shop assistant.

Kerstin: Woolworth's in general, at that time, was it considered a high quality shop?

Mary: It wasn't too bad. After the war we started getting all the imports in, getting china. When that happened, everybody was queuing up in the streets. Or if we got chocolate or something everybody would say, "Oh Woolworth's has got it." We started taking things in from Czechoslovakia, all the lovely glass and things like that. Well we didn't have that durin' the war so Woolworth's was pretty good. It was one of the first places to have nylons and things like that. If you want a little incident, when I worked in Woolworth's, when sweets came back into production after the war, I always remember, we had an assistant manager at that time, (you worked hard in these days but you were appreciated). The manager used t' come round, "How are you, how are you?" That doesn't happen nowadays and some of them would have said, "Have you got a little brother at home?" When we got a shipment of sweets and I always remember this day, we got Mars Bars. Now we'd never seen Mars Bars and the deputy manager came up with this box of Mars Bars. He said, "Now, we'll have to sell so much but I want to give the staff one bar each." I took it home and we divided it into five pieces so we could all taste a Mars Bar.

Kerstin: What about holidays?

Mary: Well, that's a joke for a start. The first year that I was there, I started in the Spring time and I qualified for three days holiday that was up to the next Spring time. And I always remember I got the last three days in November! After you'd been there for one year you qualified for one weeks holidays.

Kerstin: And what did you do in your holidays?

Mary: I went out to my Grandparents. In that days there were very few things that you could do. I went every weekend that I could but you were often workin' till eight o' clock at night in Woolworth's. I used t' help my Grandmother with the farm and the animals then I had to come back on Sunday night to start on Monday morning.

Margaret Christie: Well, I left school at fourteen and when I went to the employment bureau, you had your little report card and the lady said, "You should try to get into an office." So I went to Wordy, they were a haulage company. They had horses and carts as well. So I went there and I had an interview and they said, "We don't like staff coming and leaving quickly so if you come, you come for three months, an' if you like it an' we like you, you'll be on permanent contract after that." So for the first three months my wage was nineteen and sixpence (97.5p) which was quite a good wage for then and after the three months I got one pound ten shillings (1.50p). They were good t' work with, that was when I was fourteen. When I was eighteen they decided they wanted a comptometer operator, this was the start of the computers really. So they sent me to Edinburgh for a three week course. You had t' take all your big sheets with you and you had to calculate all the haulage and all the storage and all that sort o' thing. Then the typists had t' type out all the invoices an' everything. Then I was married and then I left cause ma father was very ill and after that, I jist had little office jobs in between having family. Although I left school at fourteen I regretted it so ma friend and I we went three nights a week to evening classes, all the shorthand, typing, business studies, book keeping, so we got a lot o' experience that way.

Coal dock worker

Andrew Pattullo born 1907.

David: When you were unemployed how did you notice the difference in your living conditions?

Andrew: Oh! Terrible, terrible, 18 bob (90p) a week. I mean, I was in lodgings at that time. I wis smoking at the time, Goldflake. The lady gave me three packets a time and at six pence (2.5p) a time, that was one and sixpence (7.5p). With one and six pence off my money for lodgings left me with fifteen bob to keep me going for a week. So I learned to stop smoking. That was back in 1937. The landlady wis very good at dishing up good meals with the meagre assistance she wis getting. It wis

Above: Coal boat ' Loch Maree' loading up at Aberdeen Harbour
Above top: Two fuel carrying lorries with Aberdeen in background.

common thing t' get porridge in the morning an' porridge at night, twice a day three times a week because that wis the only means y' hid and one thing, you got plenty soup, real soup and that's fit kept ye going. Neen o' these fancy dishes they dish oot nowadays.

David: Did you find that the food in Aberdeen was seasonal?

Andrew: Oh yes, I wouldna say that we were any worse off than anybody else, we survived.

David: So you worked for a coal company, tell me a little about it and where the coal came from.

Andrew: Most of it came from Sunderland for house coal but a lot of the steam coal came from Blyth. That wis for the trawlers more or less y' see, but most o' the trips were from Sunderland. A lot of the trawlers at that time had what you call scratch crews and instead of getting their crews from here they would put a scratch crew aboard the trawler doon by Fifeshire and they would get the boat loaded with coal and take it back to Aberdeen. The firm had certain men to do that sort of job. At that time it wis a case o' walking the plank as a lot of men called it. Y' hid a great long plank oot and you hid t' walk ower the plank with a bag of coal on your back on to the ship and then empty it into the hold of the ship y' see, and there were men in the hold trimming the coal to make room for as much as they possibly could. But later on as things advanced, they started a coaling installation and that wis far too late in coming but anyway that lasted for about ten years. Well I wis put doon there as assistant foreman for a start an' then I wis foreman but I came up just after the finish because either the boats were getting too old and being scrapped or if they were in good order, they were being converted to run on oil, so there was practically no work as far as the coal installation was concerned.

David: How was the coal taken to the harbour?

Andrew Pattullo: By boats, there wis four firms, each hid a boat. The Co-op coal hid the 'Thrift'; Aberdeen Coal and Ship Company hid the 'Red Hull' and the 'Ferryhill'; G. and A. Davidson's hid the 'Torquay' and Ellis McHardy hid the 'Spray'. The Coal Company hid jist the one the 'Red Hull' 'cause the 'Ferryhill' wis scrapped by that time. So that wis the four main firms and the four main boats that used to carry coal into Aberdeen mostly from Blyth .

Unloading coal at Aberdeen harbour.

David: So what would a normal day be like at work then?

Andrew: Oh jist like any other body. You got up in the morning. Of course we started at different times. Sometimes two o'clock in the morning, you started depending on how busy you were and you worked maybe till ten o'clock at night. Right through, you didna stop in those days. That's the reason I say my troubles are what they are now because you maybe started at two in the morning, you worked till nine o'clock in the morning. Nine to ten wis breakfast time and you come home, you were soaking, you changed your clothes, then back to work. One to two wis dinner. You were soaked again. Then you came back, changed again until maybe seven, eight, ten o'clock at night. You worked right through, carrying coal. Oh yes, you jist carried on until you'd finished your job.

David: You must have had quiet days as well?

Andrew: Oh yes y' wisna like that every day but I wouldna say it wis quiet days. Oh no, you wis busy, very busy. You wis going hell for leather every day more or less to get the boats coaled and away to sea again and that sort o' thing because there wis no let up, and o' course in these days there wis no lighting. Many a man fell into the dock. You were walking along the stick as we called it, the lang plank, and then he jist slightly lost his balance or something like that and plump right into the dock. You jist heaved him oot again. I'll give you one funny story. One lad, he wis working one Saturday afternoon and he wis a lad looking for a good bucket you see.

We got paid on a Saturday. He came back at two o'clock. 'Can I go for a pint?' 'Aye but behave yersel.' He didna come back till after three and he wis drunk by this time. So when he came back we

were sayin' 'Now don't carry because you're going to fall and hurt yersel.' Oh no, no, he would carry, he would carry. Anyway, right oh, carry on. It so happened that the plank wis level with the quay, jist a straight carry and Jim, he gets the coal on his back and walks right across. Now you see him now you don't. He walked right off the end of the stick into the water, bag of coal and everything. That sorted him out! So somebody threw out a rope til him and it so happened the rope wis greasy and he's huddin the rope and the rope's running through his fingers and he's screemin' oot of him and they finally got him oot of the water and doon into the engine room, got his clothes dried and back into his job again.

Above: Coalmen loading coal on to carts.
Above top: Carrying coal from boat to boat.

It wis a hard life, but as I said there wis a keen sense of humour and that's fit carried y' through and anither thing they used to drink quite a lot but it wis that which really kept them going. If they hidna hid a drink they would never have done the job really because the work then and the work now wis entirely different. They wouldna handle what we call the pan shovel. Oh it was a big roond shovel fit we call pan shovels. Well you hid to put six shovels into a bag of coal to make a hundred weight and a quarter. So you'll understand fit I mean. So you had to do that all day long and if there wisna enough men to do the boat, then he employed other men to do your job. Then you had to go down and coal the boats and that sort o' thing.

Painters and Decorators

John Lennox: We did six years then in our apprenticeship. I wanted to join the painters union when I became an apprentice but they said no: you waited till your last year of apprenticeship and then you joined the union. You were the boss's property when you were an apprentice. Apprentices had really no rights at all, none. Ten shillings (50p) a week was the starting wage and I ended up after six years with twenty four shillings (£1.20p) a week.

The firm I was with, Donald's did a lot of the toff's shootin' lodges up in the north east. So I spent half of my apprenticeship on country jobs. The lodgin' allowance was twelve shillin's (60p) a week. Bein' in the country you did about fifty hours a week instead o' the normal forty-four hours. That was wi' the agreement o' the trade union. You were jist paid the normal rate for that, you didnae get time and a half.

The painters bible at that time was the 'Ragged Trousered Philanthropists'. Conditions that book was describin' were familiar to me. Anyway in 1928 I got working with the firm I had served my apprenticeship with. But of course painters was a seasonal job. It was March or thereabout before you were taken on. And you could be paid off as early as July. The season could be as short as that. So we were well used to being unemployed. When a painter got paid off his world didnae collapse aboot him. That would have been the experience maybe of many other workers who'd never experienced it before. But if you were a painter you simply accepted that.

So far as Aberdeen was concerned, and the same would apply to painters in any provincial town, ye either went to Edinburgh or you went to London. It was London I went to in 1928. I went back and forth like that for a couple o' years. Then I got in with a London firm. Oh, we had many a hard time in London lookin' for work - all the different places and big furnishin' companies. They all jist had a little season and ye got in for the season and then you were paid off. In between times comin' near New Year time we hoped to get paid off - so then we came up here to Aberdeen and had an extended six weeks or thereaboot sort o' holiday at New Year. That was quite deliberate, that was how we worked it.

Finally, I got in with this London firm, Clark and Friends of Clapham. It was the time the luxury cinemas were bein' built all over the country and we went out all over wi' them. Then in 1935 I come back to Aberdeen.

Slaters

Eva Burnett: It's in the blood. They had to climb in all weathers, but they liked it. If there was a gale, we used to get police notices that there was a chimney that was unsafe, or a roof was damaged. If you got a police notice you had to say to Jimmy or Geordie, 'Will you go out and take off the chimney stack because it was a danger to the public.' It was the slater's job to take it down before it killed someone. It was a dangerous occupation, but they knew how to get out through a roof light or something. It was a three-generation firm of the same family. I went there in the war-time, and the first book I opened was for the damage done to St. Mary's Church in Carden Place. And it was for the war-damage done to the Church. Our firm had done the maintenance to the roof after the damage. I remember they did a big job, repointing St. Mary's Cathedral, and the priest came into me and said 'I want a price for re-pointing the Cathedral'. From the time that television came to Aberdeen, we were the official erectors of TV aerials. It was better for a slater to do that, for a slater knew how to walk on roofs and that. We wouldn't go on to a roof that we weren't working on in case any of the slates were 'nail-sick', that means that the nails holding the slates in place weren't galvanised, and they would rust and the slates might slip. A slater as I say, walks like a cat.

Norman: Did the equipment fail sometimes?

Eva: Well I suppose if you put up a scaffold and didn't erect it properly it would have failed. The Rosemount Terrace was the highest buildings in Aberdeen, and the boss's cousin he was up on the chimney-head and he actually 'froze'. Ye canna make a person move, once they freeze on a chimney. Well he ultimately fell down to his death, he froze because of the height, being a young chap at that time. But that was an unusual thing.

David: Did that happen frequently, people 'freezing'?

Eva: Well usually it was young people, apprentices. Again it was to do with height. Many of them would have had fathers who worked in the trade, and it was a generation thing.

I had a boss and he had about nine falls, they called him the Cat, that was his nickname, but he survived and he's in his eighties. It was a dangerous occupation, but they thought that once they were on the roof they were as safe as if they'd been on the ground.

They were never ill, you never heard of them being off with flu's and colds, whether it was because they were out in all the elements, and they were hardy. They were never off for any length of time with anything unusual, more often it was an accident. The firm that I was with, the equipment was the best that they could give.

Domestic and Nursing

Myra Hay: I left school at fourteen jist after the war. I worked in a shop in Aviemore then I came through t' Aberdeen an' worked as a domestic y'know, live in. It wis the only way country girls could come t' the town.

Trevor: Were you homesick ?

Myra: Well, yes I was until I encouraged ma sister t' come through six weeks after. So I wasn't homesick then as long as I had somebody.

Trevor: What did you think to Aberdeen coming from Aviemore ?

Myra: Well, I always remember going to the dancing an' we went to all the dances in the village an' of course we were the popular girls an' we never missed a dance. An' we went to the Abergeldie and it was a nice dance hall an' we stood an we stood an' not a soul danced wi us. It was so lonely compared wi a village dance y'know. Well as I say I was jist a domestic. That was up at 41 Queens Road. It was a home for girls, high school girls who lived in Aberdeen, I was a general dogsbody, cleaning an' things like that. I remember we lived at the very top of the building. Well that wis that an' then I got to do this trainin' t' be a nanny an' I did that for a year, then I worked in the children's nurseries, then a few years after that I got into the real nursin'.

Mrs Nicol: We had a large family, 12 of us. As soon as we were 14 we had to find work of some kind. I went into service. I went into the Hilton Hostels - a great big buildin' for students. I had two sisters who worked there as well, my sister and I, we were like table maids, housemaids. Mrs Shanks was the lady warden then, it was different days, ye had to be in by ten o'clock at night, and you weren't allowed to be out later than that. You had a half-day once in a while, and a day off once a month.

I went to work in a Norvic Shoe-shop in George Street for a few years, and then I thought I'd like to work with children, so I got a job in the childrens' department, working with children from broken homes, in Westburn Road. I was a sort of 'nurse's assistant', poor little things, sometimes the father was an alcoholic, or the parents were separated. If the father (if there was one) could afford it, he had to pay, they were asked, "How much can you afford?" they weren't drained. O, but sometimes there'd be whole families there, I remember one family, there were five children, and they had nice parents who came to see them, but the parents

Newspaper clipping highlighting the lack of domestic workers.

were 'hawkers' who couldn't afford to keep them. They lived in the Barracks in Castle Street. You had different duties for each day, and turn about. The children went to Skene Street School from Westburn Road. You'd take them to school, meet them and take them home and then back after lunch-time. They had a bath every night, got the best of food, far better than they would have got in their own homes, they had everything but love.

Industrial injuries

Archie Lennox: My mind goes back as a boy, different people I can think of who lost their eyesight in ship buildin' and the most they could ever get was a steady job so they still carried on in the same job, they'd lost their eye but they carried on just the same but I'm afraid that once the ship buildin' went down they went oot the gate jist the same as the rest.

David: What's the first thing you can remember in Grannam (Grandholm) then, the first fight that the union members put up to try and improve conditions ?

Bill Morrice: That was, one lad he worked in the —— the belts come aff y' see but they couldna stop the machine an' he lost that (half of his hand). In those days there was no compensation,

David: So he lost half of his hand 'cause he tried to put on a belt whilst the machine was still going?

Bill: Aye, an' what he got was a job for life.

David: So how many accidents did you have before they caged these things?

Bill: There was a few minor ones, y'ken, a lot o them got awar wi jist their jacket bein' torn y'ken that was ae the danger.

Man: Well, there wis serious accidents in the paper makin' industry before the union was in the mill at Culter onyway. There were two accidents at Culter that caused death. They were in the paper makin' machine the dryin' side o' it. You've t' feed it in by hand, you'd t' put it between the steel cylinders an' the felt, once the felt got hold of your hand there was no way of gettin' it out you'd actually get your neck broken before you went through the machine. And there were two cases o' that.

David: So what happened when the unions came in?

Second Man: The first chap that was killed on a paper making machine at — it was an old machine, an old machine rebuilt and it was passed by the health and safety as fit t' to make paper when it wasn't.
   And the understanding was that if the paper making machine breaks all hell breaks loose together an' the man went up to thread in an' he never come down and he'd gone straight through the cylinders. Well, he was so bad they had to get the fire brigade to get him oot wi hoses, the state he was in. An' then it happened in the next shift, I was contacted (as the branch secretary) and there was nothing we could do then, we decided to keep the other machines goin' mainly t' keep people from standin' speakin' aboot it 'cause they were worried that they would stop workin'. The firm pleaded guilty right away. I went to see the boy's mother, he was a single chap he was engaged to a girl t' get married an' they'd bought a house. I got a letter from Thompson sayin' how much his mother was goin' t' get and it was goin' to be a couple o' nothings.
   So I phoned down, it was explained, he was a single chap, he was engaged to be married, he'd bought a house so therefore he wouldn't be supportin' his mother after a certain date. What about the girl he was engaged to, well he hasn't married her so she doesn't get onything. Every one thought they were goin' t' get hundreds of thousands o' pounds but the total sum paid out was three thousand pounds.
   There's been some horrific accidents in the paper industry I'd say much more than the rest o' them in this area anyway. There were people got their hands cut off by guillotines and an arm cut aff by a guillotine and a hell o' a severe injuries where the rolls had grabbed them and jist gradually rubbin' away their fingers right doon t' their wrists some o' them, they were really horrific.

Archie: Spikin' aboot accidents, I'm goin' back to the Second World War again, and it was never recorded never knew of anything said aboot it.
   The Aberdeen trawler was the finest ship for mine sweepin' adapted in the First World War an' Hall Russell's continued to produce 'em and a terrible farce that went on for months anyway. They completed

them in their trawlin' colours an' everything, only t' be covered wi grey paint immediately they were handed over to the admiralty. That was governments movin' slowly but Hall Russell's they moved damn quick because they got onto the extent that they were launchin' 'em two at a time. They had four in a cluster an' the economy was that the two that was next to the water went off then the next two t' ging off they had the advantage to go over the side that the other lot had gone over, there was an economy in it. Once though, one o' the ships slipped off the blocks, that's an extraordinary thing you know and I always remember little Doddy Alan he was stuck underneath. Doddy was the man who had to keep the ship up and see that the ship didna fall over, slipped off the blocks. It was practically finished it only needed caulkin' an' paintin' an' it would a been ready to go inta the water. But the shipwrights had so cradled it up that it slipped off the blocks an' crushed him.

David: People I have spoken to about industrial injuries, there is always that background feeling that it is their own fault.

Man: Once you had been off with an industrial accident like I had, you claimed and got workmens' compensation, it was actually an Insurance company that you was fightin', not your employer. Being a member of a Trade Union, ye had that backing, and your Trade Union retained a solicitor, and your employer's association had a retained solicitor, but I was never in touch with the solicitors, but I was in touch with the doctors that the Master's insurance company appointed, and that was the one disappointment I got with Workmen's compensation. The attitude of medical men gave me the impression that you were malingering even though you're going about with three and a half fingers missing!

David: When you had the accident, who interviewed you? The solicitor or the doctor or both when they were working out what had happened?

Man: I was informed by the trade union secretary to go and see a doctor, but there was a lot of work done between him and the firm in Glasgow. Then they appointed a local man. When it happened that there was to be a claim, the employer's insurance company their attitude was to pay as little as possible.

Norman: You would have had experience in dealing with workmen's compensation at the slater's firm, is that right?

Eva Burnett: I can't remember if it was called ... aye that's right, 'workers' compensation'. Up to and after the war years, firms were responsible for their own insurance. I was in a slater's office, and slaters because they work on roofs, firms had to pay the highest insurance premiums, and it was 75% of the wages bill, to cover the men for accidents. If there was an accident, the insurance company was notified, and the firm got a form in to give the actual details of the accident, such as a man falling off a roof. Then through time, they would, the doctors and the insurance inspectors, would interview the man to try to come to a settlement. Well I knew one case, he was a year and a month off, and it was after that he got his settlement. And that meant me doing a year's wages back, so that they would know what a year's wages would have been for the actual settlement for the person. Whatever they got was based on the previous year's wages.

Norman: Did they concern themselves about accidents, or did they just accept that they happen sometime?

Eva: Well they accepted that accidents happen, hence the need for insurance, but if an accident happened it was never the firm's fault, it was always the worker. But there was a case where the man was off for a year and a month. He was put out on a roof on an icy day, and slaters could not go out on roofs if it was icy. He was actually putting gutters up on a two-storey granite flats. The man was up the ladder, and he put his labourer to get something from the van, and so he wasn't holding the ladder. In the trade there was always a slater and a labourer to hold the ladder. And that was part of the dispute as well, and there wasn't a settlement until after the man was fit to work. Both his legs were broken and he was badly injured.

Woman: I can understand that, if I was an employer and I'd employed a labourer to hold a ladder, I'd be annoyed if an accident happened because he was away doing something else.

Eva: Aye, but you have to remember that the labourer was also employed to assist the workman with other jobs, and you have to remember that the workman might be working 20 or 35 feet up a ladder working at something, and he shouts "Jim, I want such and such".. In all the trades it was the custom to employ a journeyman and a labourer.

David: Did you ever find that an accident like that caused a change in working practices?

Eva: I can't remember. I remember a young lad about 20 falling off a roof onto the road, (inaudible). Slaters never used to live a long life strangely enough, a lot of the slaters died before they had even reached retirement age. Whether it was the amount of falls they had, I had a boss and he had about nine falls, they called him the Cat, that was his nickname, but he survived and he's in his eighties. It was a dangerous occupation, but they thought that once they were on the roof they were as safe as if they'd been on the ground.

Bill Slater: There were two men who were on the roof cleaning the asbestos, the moss and that, then they stood up, you can see the hand rail here, (indicating the photograph) and there was a wooden platform. They had checked the platform when they went up and they realised that it needed repairs and they'd ordered new timber work from the pattern shop. They'd been taking a break and stepping back they put their hands on the handrail and the handrail gave way and of course you can see that's the glass, and they never hit the astragals and they came right down in the middle between the astragals and landed on the concrete floor. It must have been about thirty odd feet. It was a terrible thing and I will never forget it.

There was a case for it and we were fined by the health and safety people. I was general manager by that time.

STRIKES

John Lennox: Well, when I left school I was idle for six months. It was the time o' the miners' strike, 1921. And the painters in Aberdeen were also on strike. They were out for twenty one weeks. They went out for three ha'pennies (0.6p) an hour extra and unfortunately they had to settle for a ha'penny less. Then I got started my time as an apprentice painter.

The painters had a strike somewhere in about 1932 and big Sandy Bannochie, my mate, and me travelled up. I served my apprenticeship along wi' Sandy in Aberdeen. So Sandy and me did posters and was active in the strike.

(David turned to Miss B who had been involved in strike action as a hospital worker)

David: So, to survive you were having to dig into your savings. Was your husband working at the time?

Miss B: I'm not married.

David: So you were supporting yourself?

Miss B: Yes.

David asks about financial difficulties.

Peter: You hid to git it from the social work department... I think there was a hardship pay ...

Miss B: What they did actually, they only took yi out three days at a time.

David: So you just got enough to live on for the two days you were working.

Miss B: If you were over three days they hud ti pay yi, but if they only took yi out three days, the union didn't huv to pay yi.

David: So for the two days you worked were you paid by the hospital?

Miss B: Yeah, yi'd back t' work ... an then it would depend on who was taken out the ...followin' week, an then yi know it was sort ... (?)

David: So you weren't actually out constantly for a year ...

Miss B: Yi were out three days at a time ... but then the strike went over, I think everybody startit goin back actually. Because it wis a waste o time, because as I said they were losin' more money than they were gainin' anything.

SCALES OF ASSISTANCE (APPROVED 20TH FEBRUARY, 1933)

CLASSIFICATION		A Ordinary Outdoor Poor	B Unemployed Able-bodied Persons	C Transitional payments
Ordinary				
1.	Man & wife, or couple	23%	23%	23%
2.	Man, wife, and 1 dependant	25%	25%	25%
3.	Do. 2 dependants	27%	27%	27%
4.	Do. 3 do.	29%	29%	29%
5.	Do. 4 do	31%	31%	31%
6.	Do. 5 do	33%	33%	33%
7.	Do. 6 do	35%	35%	35%
Adult members in Family				
8.	If idle and over 16	7/6	7/6	7/6
9.	If working (deduct earnings)	12/6	12/6	12/6
10.	Allow actual wage if less than 12/6	12/6 or under	12/6 or under	12/6 or under
11.	Single Men and Women in Lodgings	12/6 to 15/-	12/6 to 15/-	12/6 to 15/-
Widows or Women with Children				
12.	Widow or woman and 1 dependant	15/-	15/-	15/-
13.	Do. do. 2 dependants	18/-	18/-	18/-
14.	Do. do. 3 do.	21/-	21/-	21/-
15.	Do. do. 4 do.	24/-	24/-	24/-
16.	Do. do. 5 do.	27/-	27/-	27/-
Boarded-out Children				
17.	Rate of aliment (plus extras)*	7/-	-	-
18.	Under 3 or delicate (plus extras)*	10/-	-	-
Boarded-out Mental Patients or Defectives				
19.	Rate of aliment (plus extras)*	11/-	-	-
Deductions and Allowances				
20.	National Health Insurance benefit	Normally Ignore 7/6	Ignore 7/6	Ignore 7/6
21.	Furnished rooms or sub lets	As income	As income	As income
22.	Payments from lodgers	1/4 as income	1/4 as income	1/4 as income
23.	Trade Union benefit	Ignore 5/-	Ignore 5/-	Ignore 5/-
24.	Wounds & disability pensions, money & investments, house property & compensation, in accordance with Transitional Payments (Determination of Need) Act, 1932	On merits	On merits	In accordance with Act & on merits
25.	Casual earnings	3/4 as income	3/4 as income	3/4 as income
26.	Service, Reserve, R.I.C. & all other pensions	As income	As income	As income
27.	All household income	Deducted	Deducted	Deducted
28.	Each case on its merits	On merits	On merits	-
Extras				
29.	Clothing to recipients and dependants	Discretion*	Normally nil	Nil
30.	Medical attendance & medicines	As required	In urgent cases only. Dispensary normally provides same	Nil

*ie. Clothing, boots, repairs to boots, school books (if required), medical attendance and medicines.

Top: The market in the Green
Centre: Aberdeen Harbour in the snow
Bottom: Workmen's dwellings, Urquhart Road

Acknowledgements

Betty Allen
Tony Benn
Alice Black
Eva Burnett
Harry Bygate
Gladys Christie
Margaret Christie
Alex Collie
George Cruickshank
Florence Cumming
Mat Davidson
Alec Dey
Joyce Everill
Elizabeth Findlayson
C. Gimmingham
Betty Gordon
Ellen Grant
Myra Hay
Albert Hepburn
Vera Hunter
May Hunter
Adam Jack
Jack Kilgour
Andrew Lawson
George Leiper
Archie Lennox
John Lennox
John Londragan
Ina Macintosh
Gilbert Mackland
Ina Mair
Jim McCartney
Eva Mclean
Norman Miller
Mary Milne
Stanley Milton
David Moir
Bill Morrice
Ernie Mundie
Ted Munro
Margaret Mutch
Mrs. Nicol
Andrew Pattullo
Peter Rennie
Ian Richardson
Josephine Robertson
Aileen Ross
Beatrice Sangster
Bill Shinnie
Isobel Sim
George Simpson
Mary Simpson
Bill Simpson
Bill Slater
Bill Tinto
Agnes Wallace
Isobel Wallace
Walter Watt
Jesse Watt
Sam West

And to all those who donated their reminiscences anonymously.

Special thanks to:-

Mike Dey
Fiona Gibson
Norman Miller
Gemma Milne
Jim Pratt
Kerstin Remold
Simon Spalding

Also to:- *Kaye Lawson,* for her contribution on women's enfranchisement.
          Jim Milne, as an adviser and archivist.
          Valerie Plante, for her contribution on Grandholm.

Thanks also to: *Ellis & McHardy Oils Ltd.*
                     William McKinnon.
                     The Urban Studies Centre.
                     J.M. Hendersons & Co. Ltd.

Cover painting by: *Jacek Kapocki*

Design & Layout: *Bill Smith* - *Aberdeen City Council, Publicity & Promotions Unit*

Top left: Thornton Court, Guestrow - 1927
Bottom left: Aberdeen Harbour - 1960s
Right: Manufacturing cloth - 1940s

WORK, *Welfare* the *Price* of FISH

From top to bottom:
Washing and cleaning on a trawler
Through the breakwater at Aberdeen harbour
A granite saw in operation
Two working horses

Above left: The Town House, overlooking the Guestrow area, 1920's
Above right: Spa Street in the mid 1920's
Left: Union Street at the St.Nicholas Street/ Market Street junction, 1950's
Below: Staff of the Northern Co-op Dairy, Berryden, 1928

WORK, Welfare & the Price of FISH

Some of the contributers - Above left: L to R Ted Munro, Bill Moir, Joyce Everill, Jim Mitchell and Jim Robertson
Above right: Ted Munro and Alex Collie

Back cover - Main picture: Aberdeen trawler "Loch Lomond" aground on the North Pier platform
Bottom - Left: The Castlegate market   Centre: Fresh Fish staff, Allen and Dey   Right: Demolition in the Rosemount area

The Wallace Tower (Blenholm's Lodge)
in its original site on the corner of
Netherkirkgate and Carnagie's Brae.
The building was moved to its present site
on Tillydrone Road, Old Aberdeen in 1965.